THE OFFICIAL

HANDBOOK OF THE

VAST
RIGHT-WING
CONSPIRACY

THE OFFICIAL
HANDBOOK OF THE
VAST
RIGHT-WING
CONSPIRACY

THE ARGUMENTS YOU NEED
TO DEFEAT THE LOONY LEFT

MARK W. SMITH

Since 1947
REGNERY
PUBLISHING, INC.
An Eagle Publishing Company • Washington, DC

Library of Congress Cataloging-in-Publication Data

Smith, Mark W., 1968–
    The official handbook of the vast right-wing conspiracy /
    Mark W. Smith.
       p. cm.
    ISBN 0-89526-085-9 (pbk. : alk. paper)
  1. Conservatism—United States. 2. Right and left (Political
science) I. Title.
    JC573.2.U6S644 2004
    320.52'0973—dc22

                                    2004004047

Published in the United States by
Regnery Publishing, Inc.
An Eagle Publishing Company
One Massachusetts Avenue, NW
Washington, DC 20001

Visit us at www.regnery.com

Distributed to the trade by
National Book Network
4720-A Boston Way
Lanham, MD 20706

Printed on acid-free paper

Manufactured in the United States of America

10 9 8 7 6 5 4 3 2 1

Books are available in quantity for promotional or premium use. Write to Director of Special Sales, Regnery Publishing, Inc., One Massachusetts Avenue, NW, Washington, DC 20001, for information on discounts and terms, or call (202) 216-0600.

To my mother, Joan H. Smith,
and to the memory of my father, Warren B. Smith.

Also to the memory of General Joseph Warren,
who gave his life for American liberty
at the Battle of Bunker Hill, June 17, 1775.

CONTENTS

FIND YOUR
VAST RIGHT-WING
CONSPIRACY RATING

Are you Hillary's worst nightmare—a member of the Vast Right-Wing Conspiracy? I mean, a *card-carrying* member?

★ ★ ★ ★ ★

We Conspiracy members have much to be cheerful about. Since the 1980s, Americans have become steadily more conservative. Slick Willie himself bequeathed to a grateful nation Republican control of the White House, the Senate, *and* the House of Representatives. Add to that the meteoric rise of FOX News Channel, the domination of talk radio and the bestseller lists by conservatives, and only a tie-dye-wearing Naderite true believer would have any trouble seeing which way the wind is blowing. Even some former knee-jerk liberal jerks have seen the light—like comedian Dennis Miller—and have moved their acts to the right.

But just because the nation has moved to the right does not mean that anyone who calls himself a Republican, or even a conservative, necessarily qualifies as a member of the Conspiracy. Senators Arlen Specter of Pennsylvania, Olympia Snow of Maine, and Lincoln Chafee of Rhode Island may be Republicans, but hardly Conspiracy members. Liberal

New York City mayor Michael Bloomberg? Not in the Conspiracy.

Democrats have tried to get in on the action too: Some like to get their photographs taken while holding guns or while hunting. Others talk about being war heroes in their youth, only to later refuse to defend the country—think John Kerry and George McGovern. But true members of the Vast Right-Wing Conspiracy are not fooled. Presidential hopefuls like Howard Dean mistakenly think they are nestling up to Conspiracy members by talking about "guys with Confederate flags on their pickup trucks." But they are not Conspiracy members.

True members of the Conspiracy support less government, lower taxes, free markets, private property rights, and a strong national defense. Conspiracy members support the U.S. Constitution as envisioned by the Founding Fathers (not as envisioned by elite law professors or liberal judges). Conspiracy members don't have problems admitting that they love America and certainly don't care about Kofi Annan and his merry band of petty tyrants at the UN. Conspiracy members don't light candles to express sadness at the execution of a rapist and murderer, but instead offer to pull the switch themselves. Conspiracy members support the right to own a gun, the right to use the word "God" in the Pledge of Allegiance, and do not shudder in fear when they see a Nativity scene conspicuously placed in a public park.

So let's find out just how right-wing you really are by taking this quick test:

1. **The person best qualified to choose my doctor, my child's teacher, what to eat, and whether I should smoke is:**

   A. Hillary.
   B. Hillary's village.
   C. Me.

2. **When shopping, I am most likely to make an impulse buy of:**

   A. a John Kerry plush toy.
   B. a $55 Hillary Clinton T-shirt by Marc Jacobs.
   C. an Ann Coulter action figure.

3. **Fill in the blank: The government that governs _____, governs best.**

   A. everything
   B. with the most compassion
   C. least

4. **Who was the best president of the last thirty years?**

   A. The Man from Hope.
   B. Hmm, I can't decide between Jimmy Carter and Gerald Ford.
   C. Reagan for Rushmore!

5. **Which nations should have nukes?**

   A. None. You can't hug with nuclear arms.
   B. The UN should decide.
   C. The U.S. and its allies.

6. Who should own guns in America?

   A. Good heavens, no one should. Guns kill.

   B. Only the governing authorities, since they know what's best for us.

   C. Any red-meat-eating, law-abiding citizen who chooses to do so.

7. Fill in the blank: Taxes should be _____.

   A. high. Don't you have any compassion for the poor?

   B. cut, but not for the rich.

   C. low. A worker has a right to enjoy the fruits of his labors.

8. Before America takes any more military action in the war on terror, we should:

   A. make sure it's okay with the UN.

   B. try to understand what we have done to make the poor terrorists hate us.

   C. develop even more sophisticated and deadly weapons.

9. The military budget should be:

   A. cut. Let the military hold a bake sale to buy a bomber.

   B. submitted to the UN for approval.

   C. as high as it needs to be to repel threats to our nation.

10. What makes you angry?

    A. People who would rather buy an SUV than a VW bug.

    B. The fact that the world is not ordered the way
       Hillary and the Harvard University faculty think it
       should be ordered.

    C. People who don't work, but live off the taxpayers.

11. Which phrase best describes your beliefs?

    A. Al Gore was a brilliant policy genius (and really
       funny on *Saturday Night Live*).

    B. Lying under oath about sex doesn't matter.

    C. Individual freedom and personal responsibility pave
       the road to success.

**12. Who gave you your right to life, liberty, and the
pursuit of happiness?**

    A. The ACLU.

    B. The Supreme Court.

    C. The Creator.

The more often you answered "C," the more truly you
are a member of the Vast Right-Wing Conspiracy. If you
want to improve your rating or are just looking for more
ammo to combat the liberal lunacy that bleats out from
Dan Rather, Peter Jennings, and the *New York Times*, this
book will help you.

The Official Handbook of the Vast Right-Wing Conspiracy,
I am proud to say with all the modesty of Rush Limbaugh,
synthesizes the best of conservative thought. It is brief and
to the point, because Americans are busy people—especially conservatives, who actually have jobs and families to
support. It gives you a concise guide to the conservative

take on issues—perfect as ammunition for conservatives and education for prospective converts to the Conspiracy. Armed with *The Official Handbook of the Vast Right-Wing Conspiracy*, you'll be able nimbly and eloquently to win political discussions with friends, family, and Al Franken. In a few short hours, this book could transform Barbra Streisand into Ann Coulter.

I am not trying to reinvent the wheel here. This book is a portable distillation of the essential ideas and arguments of notable conservatives like James Madison, Ronald Reagan, Rush Limbaugh, Thomas Sowell, Walter Williams, and hundreds of other right-thinking authors and scholars. I wrote it to give you sound bites for this evening's cocktail party, your next college class, or your first appearance on *The O'Reilly Factor*.

One final bonus: Once you master the arguments in *The Official Handbook*, Hillary will kick you out of her village—forever.

NO LIBERAL MEDIA BIAS? LET'S GET REAL

How can the press report politics objectively when 89 percent of the Washington bureau chiefs and reporters voted for Bill Clinton in 1992, while only 7 percent voted for George Bush? Of note, only 43 percent of Americans voted for Bill Clinton.[1]

★　★　★　★　★

Here's what the liberals say. . .

LIBERAL LUNACY:
"Because the media is dominated by for-profit businesses run largely by white males, they're really conservative and represent corporate interests."

This one is really a whopper. First, "corporate America" is not necessarily conservative. The federal government's antitrust lawsuit against Microsoft was encouraged by "corporate America" in the form of companies like Netscape.[2] Second, "corporate America" is hardly a monolithic entity. Liberals label any business trying to make a profit as part of "corporate America." This is false.

In fact, "corporate America" has lots of rabid liberals in its ranks. New Jersey's liberal senator Jon Corzine, New York City Republican-In-Name-Only mayor Michael Bloomberg, investor Warren Buffet, CNN's founder Ted Turner, and of course Bush-hating investor George Soros are all rich white males running corporate America, but they're hardly card-carrying members of the vast right-wing conspiracy.

Liberals also ignore that the owners of the large media companies are not the ones producing and directing the content of what appears on television and in print. That's left to the liberals running the news desks and the lefty producers who decide which segments to air. Liberal anchors such as Dan Rather, Tom Brokaw, and Peter Jennings prove the point.

No liberal media bias? Then why did *Newsweek*, which had a tape of a young female intern discussing her affair with the president of the United States, decide not to go with the story? Maybe because it would reflect poorly on a Democratic president? (Instead, the Monica Lewinsky story was broken on the Internet by the Drudge Report.)[3]

> ❝ I think most newspapermen by definition have to be liberal; if they're not liberal, by my definition of it, they can hardly be good newspapermen. ❞
>
> —Walter Cronkite, former CBS News anchor

How can the press report politics objectively when 89 percent of the Washington bureau chiefs and reporters voted for Bill Clinton in 1992, while only 7 percent voted for George H. W. Bush? Only 43 percent of all Americans voted for Bill Clinton.[4]

The media's conduct in the 2000 presidential election proves its liberal bias. Throughout election night 2000, the networks publicly called states for Gore much sooner than they called states for Bush—even though the margin of victory was greater in the pro-Bush states than in the pro-Gore states.[5] In *At Any Cost*, White House correspondent Bill Sammon reviewed the media's election night coverage. He found that Gore won Michigan by four points and was awarded the state by CNN the instant the first polls closed—even though voters in western Michigan still had another hour to vote. Bush won Ohio by the same margin, four points, but it took an hour and forty-five minutes for CNN to award the state to Bush. Gore won Illinois by twelve points and CNN named him the winner in one minute; Bush won Georgia by twelve points and CNN waited thirty-three minutes.

Even more amazingly, Ann Coulter points out in *Slander* that "the Associated Press called Florida for Gore even though its own internal numbers had Bush winning—but refused to call Florida for Bush later in the evening when both its internal numbers and the [Voter News Services] numbers showed Bush the winner."[6]

LIBERAL LUNACY:
"Conservatives dominate the all-powerful FOX News Channel and the waves of talk radio, whose influence overwhelms any liberals in media."

Oh, really? So I guess we can just ignore the liberal bias of ABC, NBC, CBS, CNN, and PBS, as well as virtually all of the major daily newspapers in the nation. Before the rise of talk radio, the Internet, and FOX News Channel, conservatives were inundated by liberal propaganda. The purported "newspaper of record," the *New York Times,* hasn't endorsed a Republican presidential candidate since Dwight Eisenhower. That's right: The *Times* endorsed George McGovern in 1972, Walter Mondale in 1984, and Michael Dukakis in 1988, as well as Jimmy Carter twice (1976 and 1980), Bill Clinton twice (1992 and 1996), and Al Gore (2000).

The rise of FOX News has given some balance to the media's overwhelmingly liberal tilt. Unfortunately, despite its success, FOX News is still not available in all areas of the country. When compared to the number of viewers that NBC, CBS, ABC, and CNN reach every night, FOX's supposedly all-powerful influence pales in comparison.

Before FOX News, talk radio was virtually conservatives' only recourse. Conservatives dominate talk radio because people listen to them. There is no "liberal version of Rush Limbaugh" because nobody wants to listen to liberals. Liberals who have started radio shows only to have them canceled due to lack of listener interest include former New York governor Mario Cuomo, former Texas agriculture commissioner Jim Hightower, Harvard Law professor Alan Dershowitz, former presidential candidate Gary Hart, former Connecticut governor Lowell Weicker, former New York Democratic mayor Ed Koch, former California Democratic governor Jerry Brown, and former Virginia Democratic governor Douglas Wilder.

In contrast, the radio waves are full of successful conservatives, including Rush Limbaugh, Oliver North, Matt Drudge, Michael Reagan, Michael Savage, Bill O'Reilly, Laura Ingraham, and Sean Hannity—to name just a few. Sidestepping the liberal stranglehold on the major media, these talented conservatives give people a consumer choice. And when the American people are given a choice, they choose conservative.

LIBERAL LUNACY:
"But conservatives get hired to air their views in the major media."

Nope. When they get on at all, conservatives still have to go to the back of the bus. Sure, a handful of conservatives may get to appear on the major networks, but only as clearly labeled "conservative commentators"—not as plain ol' "objective reporters." You won't catch the major networks giving a conservative a slot to deliver hard, objective news.

So while George Stephanopoulos, one of Bill Clinton's top advisors, was hired by ABC as the host of *This Week*, conservatives such as Pat Buchanan, George Will, Tucker Carlson, and John McLaughlin are always boxed into "reserved" or "designated" conservative seats.

In her eye-opening book *Slander*, Ann Coulter supplies an impressive list of former Democratic staffers who appear on television as "objective" news purveyors. The list includes, among many others, NBC's Tim Russert, who worked for New York Democratic governor Mario Cuomo and Democratic senator Daniel Patrick Moynihan; CNN's Jeff Greenfield, who was a speechwriter for Democratic senator Bobby Kennedy and liberal New York mayor John Lindsay; and CNBC's Chris Matthews, who wrote speeches for Jimmy Carter and Reagan nemesis Tip O'Neill. PBS's Bill Moyers worked as President Lyndon B. Johnson's press secretary. None of these people are labeled "liberal" commentators; instead, they're presented as "genuinely objective" journalists. Conservatives don't get that kind of respect.

LIBERAL LUNACY:
"Even if journalists vote for Democrats, it does not mean that they unfairly report the news."

A great example of how the liberal media reports stories biased against politically conservative views is how they report stories about gun control. The public policy organization Media Research Center conducted a study tracking for two years in the late 1990s how the major media reported on gun issues. The study found that of the 653 gun-policy stories broadcast, 357 stories tilted in favor of gun control while a mere thirty-six tilted against gun control. That's an anti-gun bias of ten to one.[7] Likewise, John R. Lott, Jr. explained that in 2001, the three major television networks—NBC, CBS, and ABC—ran 190,000 words worth of gun crime stories on their morning and evening national news broadcasts. But they ran not a single story mentioning a private citizen using a gun to stop a crime. The print media was almost as biased: The *New York Times* ran 50,745 words on contemporaneous gun crimes, but only one short, 163-word story on a retired police officer who used his gun to stop a robbery. For *USA Today*, the tally was 5,660 words on gun crimes versus zero on defensive uses.[8]

VRWC TALKING POINTS

Despite ridiculous liberal pretensions to the contrary, the majority of media in America is overwhelmingly biased to the left—and they distort the "news" and "facts" that Americans see every day. Consider:

★ Eighty-nine percent of the Washington bureau chiefs and reporters voted for Bill Clinton in 1992 while only 7 percent voted for George Bush.

★ The *New York Times* has not endorsed a Republican presidential candidate since Dwight Eisenhower in the 1950s.

★ On the major networks, conservatives fill slots as the token conservative commentators on Sunday morning talk shows, but liberals are hired as anchors and hosts to deliver hard, objective news.

THE WAR ON TERROR: YES, VIRGINIA, MILITANT ISLAMISTS DO WANT TO KILL US

Militant Islamists have repeatedly declared war on America, burning American flags, burning American presidents in effigy, shouting "Death to America," calling us the "Great Satan," and carrying out terrorist attacks against American citizens around the world. Isn't it time we take them at their word?

★ ★ ★ ★ ★

Here's what the liberals say. . .

LIBERAL LUNACY:
"Islam is a religion of peace. It is racist and wrong to suggest that the terrorists have anything to do with true Islam."

I smell something. Did someone just bring a red herring in here? Sure, most Muslims aren't terrorists. But we didn't see any Amish farmers, Israeli Jews, Buddhists, or Lutherans perpetrating or celebrating the mass murder of three thousand people on 9/11. Only Militant Islamists celebrated. Liberals can walk around telling themselves that this is not a holy war, but the Militant Islamists obviously did not get the memo.

There is a good reason for this. These terrorists think they're fighting an Islamic jihad, just as Muslims have done since the seventh century. In the radical Muslim view, Islam is a religion of peace only for those who believe in and follow the Qur'an—especially parts like what Muslims know as the Verse of the Sword, for which Osama has praised Allah in one of his communiqués. You know the one: it goes, "Slay the unbelievers wherever you find them" (Qur'an, Sura 9:5).

Renowned Islamic scholar Bernard Lewis explains, "One of the basic tasks bequeathed to Muslims by the Prophet [Muhammad] was jihad." Lewis says that the "overwhelming majority of early authorities, citing the relevant passages of the [Qur'an], the commentaries, and the traditions of the Prophet, discuss jihad in military terms. According to Islamic law, it is lawful to wage war against . . . infidels [and] apostates" and that such a jihad is "a religious obligation."

That means that Marin County's John Walker Lindh (aka Abdul Hamid), the kid from California who converted to Islam and ended up fighting with the Taliban against American troops, was only doing what he thought Allah wanted him to do. So was Osama himself on 9/11. So are the thousands upon thousands of members of Islamic terrorist groups around the world today.

To Militant Islamists, if you're with the program, you're okay. But if not, then you're either an apostate or an infi-

> **CONVERSATION STOPPER**
>
> Only Militant Islamists celebrated the mass murder of three thousand people on 9/11. Liberals can tell themselves that this is not a holy war, but the Militant Islamists obviously did not get the memo.

del, and deserve to be killed. As a non-Muslim nation, America can expect about as much peace from the Militant Islamists as was given to the huge, ancient Buddha statues in Afghanistan—destroyed by the Taliban in 2001 in the name of Islamic purity.

Bottom line: The U.S. is at war. The threat we face today from Militant Islam is no different (except in name and philosophical foundation) than the previous threats we faced from the racial fascism of Nazism and the economic fascism of Communism.

We're not saying U.S. foreign policy is perfect. But there is nothing about U.S. foreign policy that can excuse the action of the Militant Islamic terrorists. The U.S. may be mad at France, but does this give us the right to blow up the Eiffel Tower? The radical Islamists and their supporters in the West who attribute terrorism to U.S. foreign policy are simply putting up a smoke screen.

How is it that liberals, who have found in the Constitution—voila!—unexpressed "individual rights" to abortion, sodomy, and Miranda warnings, suddenly turn a blind eye to the clear nature and motives of the terrorists who are seeking our destruction? We didn't ask for a religious war or a clash of civilizations, but that's just what the radical Muslims are fighting. If we don't defend ourselves, we will lose.

LIBERAL LUNACY:
"9/11 was caused by America's arrogant foreign policy. America needs to stop angering the 'Arab street.'"

The world toward which the Militant Islamists strive cannot peacefully coexist with the Western world. The Western world is based upon the belief that ordinary people should have the opportunity to make their own life choices for themselves and their families. In stark contrast, Militant Islamic leaders want to create a world in which they make the life decisions for their subjects to best advance the views of Allah and Muhammad.

Islamists would be trying to destroy the U.S. even if we withdrew all our troops from everywhere in the world tomorrow and stopped making any statement at all about foreign affairs. Want proof? Consider this: Osama bin Laden didn't say even one word about U.S. policy toward Israel and the Palestinians until after 9/11, although he had had plenty to say about how evil we were before then.

Anyway, it wouldn't matter if the U.S. really were the global terrorist state that the Left (along with radical Muslims) likes to pretend it is: No matter how valid any complaints against the U.S. may be, nothing can justify terrorist attacks against innocent, unarmed civilians. No matter why terrorists chose to bring down the Twin Towers, they did so. Now we have to defend ourselves and destroy them. This is war.

When 9/11 happened, the Blame-America-First crowd, which had been relatively quiet since the collapse of the Soviet Union, was back in force. Reality check: 9/11 was not our fault. It was the direct result not of what the U.S. has done, but of what we are. Militant Islamists do not hate us for anything more than who we are: a tolerant, religiously diverse, and free society. We pose a threat to their vision of utopia on Earth simply because we do not all bow to Mecca several times a day.

Our free society has made us the envy of the world, as well as the world's preeminent nation militarily, economically, and culturally. But radical Muslims resent our global superiority. They're looking for ways to knock us down a peg. They delight in criticizing our decadence and immorality—although these same Islamic moralists were deafeningly silent about the morality in the rape and torture of Saddam Hussein's prisoners. Nor did they have much to say about the palaces Saddam built with emergency aid money meant for Iraq's civilians.

Let's get something straight: The U.S. is the most generous nation in the world. American taxpayers shell out between $6 and $9 billion in foreign aid each year. Muslim countries get a great deal of this—Egypt alone sucks up over $2 billion a year. And if America didn't buy any oil, Arab states would be even worse off than they are now (and would probably be getting even more American billions in aid). Meanwhile, presidents since Jimmy Carter have tried to mediate a just settlement of the Israeli-Palestinian dispute—one that would be fair to both sides (despite the fact that doing so would reward the Palestinians for their terrorist attacks). In 2000, the U.S. elected a president who supports the creation of a Palestinian (i.e., Arab Muslim) state to help resolve the Israel-Palestinian stalemate. In the 1990s, the U.S. helped rescue Muslims in the Balkans from "ethnic cleansing" by Serbs. Also in the 1990s, the U.S. tried to feed starving Somalis—leading to the "Black Hawk Down" debacle, which claimed the lives of eighteen American soldiers. In the 1980s, the U.S. helped Muslims fighting in Afghanistan against the Soviet Union.

What did the U.S. get in return for these efforts? We got 9/11. Weakness, generosity, concessions and appeasement have only emboldened the terrorists. Islamic militants are not moved by our good intentions, earnest efforts, and charity—to them, anyone who is not in the House of Islam must be destroyed.

LIBERAL LUNACY:
"To gain political advantage over the Democrats, President Bush is lying to the American public by exaggerating the threat posed by terrorism."

Ted Kennedy said this one. Ted, do you really think President Bush's work to defend the country is one big "fraud"? Do you think those planes flying into the World Trade Center were just Hollywood props? Tell that to any American who lost a loved one on 9/11. Tell it to Lisa Beamer and to the child who will never know her heroic father.

Look into their eyes, Ted. Tell them that avenging the deaths of their loved ones is a fraud. Tell them that fighting to prevent future attacks is a cynical attempt to gain political advantage. What do you think they will say?

After spending eight years defending the self-indulgent and nihilistic Clinton administration, liberals may not be able to believe that an American president could be motivated by anything but cynical, calculating self-aggrandizement. They've forgotten that the government's primary purpose is actually to defend the country (no, Hillary, not to tell us how to live our lives and raise our children). 9/11 and the almost-daily terrorist attacks against Israel (the only Western-style democracy in the Middle East) make it mind-boggling that anyone would claim that the terrorist threat is exaggerated.

In reality, conservatives understate the threat. Though the terrorists may lack the military, economic, and technological means to destroy the West, their use of modern technology gives them the capacity to inflict catastrophic casualties. Make no mistake: If al Qaeda or any other terrorist organization had had a nuclear weapon on 9/11, they would have used it. Then the left-wing talking heads at the *New York Times* wouldn't even be here to question the president's motives.

VRWC TALKING POINTS

Militant Islamists divide the world into two houses—the House of Peace, which includes the followers of "true" Islam, and the House of War, the rest of us apostates and infidels who do *not* follow "true" Islam. Militant Islamists want to destroy those in the House of War. Guess where we fall?

* In the last decade, Militant Islamists have repeatedly attacked Americans and American interests here and abroad, culminating in the three thousand murders and $1 trillion in economic losses inflicted by the 9/11 attacks.

* No Amish farmers, Israeli Jews, Buddhists, or Lutherans were seen perpetrating or celebrating the mass murder of three thousand people on 9/11. Only Militant Islamists were seen celebrating.

* Unlike liberals, conservatives learned the lessons of 9/11 and heard the clarion call of war from the Militant Islamists. In contrast, liberals have not internalized the message of 9/11, i.e., that we are at war against Militant Islamists and they fully intend to kill us—if we let them.

* The Militant Islamists and the lunatic variant of the Islamic religion must be destroyed. If we lose this war, no other political issue will matter, for a free society cannot survive with suicide bombers blowing up malls, offices, and theaters. Allowing the Islamist terrorist network to expand and grow would result in the destruction of our way of life.

THE WAR IN IRAQ:
SADDAM HAD IT COMING

Why do liberals oppose "regime change" in Iraq? Would liberals have opposed "regime change" in Hitler's Germany? In Stalin's Soviet Union? In Pol Pot's Cambodia?

★ ★ ★ ★ ★

Here's what the liberals say. . .

LIBERAL LUNACY:
"Like all wars, the war in Iraq didn't solve anything."

From Haight-Ashbury to Greenwich Village, from UC-Berkeley to Harvard Yard, the cry resounds: "Oh, if only we had given peace a chance!" War, they tell us, is never the answer—not in Iraq, not anywhere.

Is that so? Let's see. The Civil War killed 600,000 Americans. World War I killed nine million people. World War II killed fifty million. But the question isn't, "Did lots of people die?" The question is, "Did these wars make any positive difference?"

Well, after the Civil War slavery was eliminated. Four million African-American slaves became free citizens. Was war justified to free the slaves? Are Europe and Asia better off today with the defeat of Nazism, Fascism, and Japanese imperialism? It's an unpleasant fact, but sometimes you need to make war to have peace.

LIBERAL LUNACY:
"No blood for oil!"

In reality, the Iraq invasion had little to do with oil. If the U.S. simply wanted to use war to get free or cheaper oil, we could have kept Kuwait's oil fields for ourselves back in 1991. Heck, in 1991 the U.S. could have moved its 550,000 troops on the ground into Iraq itself to capture the oil fields; after all, Iraq had no army left to oppose us. Who could have stopped us? Why have we been paying market prices for Kuwaiti and Iraqi oil ever since?

If America wants to use its military might just to conquer or to steal oil, then why don't we move southward and seize the Mexican or Venezuelan oil fields? It would be a whole lot cheaper to take oil fields south of the border than to send our carrier groups halfway around the world. Besides, if all we wanted was cheaper oil, the U.S. would've simply given into French and German demands to lift the economic sanctions on Iraq in the 1990s.

> **CONVERSATION STOPPER**
>
> If the U.S. wanted to use military might to conquer and steal oil, it would have been a lot cheaper to seize Mexican or Venezuelan oil fields.

Anyway, as author Ann Coulter said it best: "Why not go to war for oil? We need oil." How else do we expect to keep the lights, refrigerators, and cars running? Don't we want our homes heated in the winter and cooled in the summer?

LIBERAL LUNACY:
"Saddam was no real threat."

Make no mistake: Choosing "peace" in Iraq would have been choosing Saddam, whose regime was a criminal mob masquerading as a government. This mob regime executed between 300,000 and one million Iraqis. Rape, torture, and murder were national policies. Saddam started a war with Iran in which one to 1.5 million people died. During it, he used poison gas on Iranian soldiers in violation of the Geneva Convention. Saddam invaded Kuwait and seized its oil fields in 1991. He also used poison gas against Iraq's unarmed Kurdish population.

Saddam has also supported worldwide terrorism. To encourage suicide bombings in Israel, Saddam gave up to $25,000 to families of Palestinian suicide bombers who murdered civilians on buses and in restaurants.[1] He sheltered members of the Abu Nidal Organization and the Palestine Liberation Front (PLF), a group headed by Abu Abbas. Remember him? He was the leader of the band that hijacked the cruise ship *Achille Lauro* in 1985 and murdered a wheelchair-bound U.S. citizen, Leon Klinghoffer.

LIBERAL LUNACY:
"We haven't found WMDs, so Saddam didn't have any."

There's no dispute—even from the United Nations or the Democratic party—that Saddam possessed and actually used weapons of mass destruction. Between 1984 and 1988, six separate teams of UN investigators documented instances of Iraq using chemical weapons on Iranians. In

1988, the Security Council blamed Iraq for using mustard gas in attacks against Iranian cities. The same year, Iraqi foreign minister Tariq Aziz openly admitted that poison gas was enshrined in official Iraqi war policy.

Saddam also tried to develop chemical weapons. Gaps identified by UNSCOM in Iraqi accounting and current production capabilities strongly suggested that Iraq maintained stockpiles of chemical agents: probably VX, sarin, cyclosarin, and mustard gas. Iraq failed to account for hundreds of tons of chemical precursors and tens of thousands of unfilled munitions, including Scud-variant missile warheads. Nor has it accounted for about 550 artillery shells filled with mustard agent.[2]

What's more, Saddam tried to acquire nuclear weapons technology. With the help of his pals in France, Saddam built the Osirik nuclear reactor, which would have given him access to the materials he needed for a nuclear weapon. Fortunately, Israel destroyed the reactor in a 1981 bombing raid (which was, incidentally, condemned widely at the time).

LIBERAL LUNACY:
"George Bush lied about WMDs
and the dangers posed by Saddam."

So, President Bush conspired with British prime minister Tony Blair, Secretary of State Colin Powell, Secretary of Defense Donald Rumsfeld, and the American and British military and intelligence services to fabricate reasons for invading Iraq? Yet no one in this grand conspiracy remembered to plant some anthrax somewhere?

If Bush really fabricated the evidence about WMDs before the war, as some liberals claim, wouldn't he have been deceptive enough to have also planted evidence of

How have things in Iraq improved since President Bush's speech aboard the USS *Lincoln* in May 2003?[4]

- Saddam has been caught.

- 60,000 Iraqis have been trained and are providing security for Iraqi civilians.

- Most of Iraq's court system is operating.

- Power generation has hit 4,518 megawatts, exceeding the prewar average.

- Iraq's universities and colleges are open, as are most primary and secondary schools.

- About 240 hospitals and over 1,200 health clinics are open.

- Over 22 million vaccination doses have been administered to Iraqi children.

- Iraq has a single, unified currency (without Saddam's picture on it) for the first time in fifteen years.

- Saddam's Ministry of Information has been replaced with about 200 private newspapers.

WMDs? If President Bush were that sinister, then how hard would it have been to have someone drop a vial of anthrax in a Baghdad basement? Saddam had left the world with no choice but to assume he had them.

Remember, the U.S.-led coalition stopped fighting the 1991 Persian Gulf War only because Saddam agreed not only to give up his WMD programs, but also to bear the burden of proving that he in fact did so. The burden to prove that Saddam had no WMDs fell upon Saddam himself. Yet, Saddam never came close to satisfying this burden, for he repeatedly lied for a decade about his internal weapons development and even kicked out UN weapons inspectors from Iraq in 1998. We know that Saddam developed and used WMDs because he used them against both the Iranians and the Kurds.

According to the Interim Progress Report delivered to Congress in October 2003, investigators in Iraq have already located dozens of WMD-related program activities and large amounts of equipment that Iraq concealed from UN weapons inspectors, as well as strains of biological organisms that could be used to make biological weapons (concealed in a scientist's home).

And even more recently, we learned from David Kay, former head of the Iraqi Survey Group, that the evidence of Saddam's intent to acquire WMDs is undis-puted. In his January 2004 testimony before the U.S. Senate, Kay explained that Saddam, in violation of UN resolutions, had a

---

In 1998, a far-sighted politician said:

❝ [We] gave Saddam a chance, not a license. If we turn our backs on his defiance, the credibility of U.S. power as a check against Saddam will be destroyed. We will not only have allowed Saddam to shatter the inspection system that controls his weapons of mass destruction; we will also have fatally undercut the fear of force that stops Saddam from acting to gain domination of the region.[5] ❞

Who said it? Bill Clinton.

missile program that had the potential to incorporate WMDs in their warheads.

According to Kay, UN inspectors had found enormous quantities of banned chemical and biological weapons in Iraq in the 1990s and that Saddam "certainly could have produced small amounts" of chemical and biological weapons. He even went so far as to conclude that Iraq "was in the early stages of renovating [Iraq's nuclear weapon program]." He also noted that "[t]here's absolutely no doubt" that, if still in power, Saddam would harbor ambitions to develop and use WMDs. Kay agreed that toppling Saddam was wholly justified and, in doing so, the security of the United States and the world was enhanced.

> ❝The world is far safer with the disappearance and the removal of Saddam Hussein. I have said I actually think this may be one of those cases where it was even more dangerous than we thought. I think when we have the complete record you're going to discover that after 1998 it became a regime that was totally corrupt. Individuals were out for their own protection. And in a world where we know others are seeking WMDs, the likelihood at some point in the future of a seller and a buyer meeting up would have made that a far more dangerous country than even we anticipated with what may turn out to be a fully accurate estimate. ❞
>
> —David Kay, former head of the Iraqi Survey Group

Going to war for the "wrong" reasons does not necessarily make the war unjust. The original reason President Abraham Lincoln fought the U.S. Civil War was to "preserve the Union"—not to free the slaves. Yet, we look back at the Civil War as a just war because it freed the slaves. Likewise, in Iraq, the freeing of twenty-six million

Iraqis from the tyranny of Saddam makes that cause just regardless of the WMD issue.

Let's also not forget exactly who is responsible for configuring the current "intelligence community." It was Bill Clinton whose policies decimated American intelligence during the 1990s, so if anyone is to blame for poor intelligence, then blame Clinton.

LIBERAL LUNACY:
"We should have given the UN more time."

Think we should have waited for the UN? The UN had its chance—twelve years. A better question: Why didn't the UN act? Saddam Hussein repeatedly violated sixteen United Nations Security Council Resolutions by, among other things, "continuing to seek and develop chemical, biological, and nuclear weapons, and prohibited long-range missiles; brutalizing the Iraqi people, including committing gross human rights violations and crimes against humanity; supporting international terrorism; refusing to release or account for prisoners of war and other missing individuals from the Gulf War era; refusing to return stolen Kuwaiti property; and working to circumvent the UN's economic sanctions."[6]

Saddam had twelve years to prove that he had disarmed. He didn't do it. Only when U.S. Navy carrier battle groups showed up on his doorstep in early 2003 did he destroy a handful of illegal missiles—which he had previously denied even having. Then we discovered that Saddam had illegal drone airplanes capable of distributing poison gas or biological agents. Clearly, if Saddam was even remotely serious about giving up his most deadly weapons, he had plenty of chances to do so before our troops pulled him out of his rabbit hole.

Remember, liberals love to give unelected, unaccountable government bureaucrats more time, money, and resources to perform jobs that they have previously failed to perform. This is true with the government's failed war on poverty, failing public school systems, and now with the UN in Iraq.

VRWC TALKING POINTS

There's no dispute—even from the UN or the Democratic Party—that Saddam possessed and actually used weapons of mass destruction. The American Left pretends to care about international human rights yet decided to oppose the military ouster of one of the most tyrannical dictators of the twentieth century. Consider:

* Saddam executed between 300,000 and one million Iraqis.

* In 1995, Hussein Kamal, Saddam's son-in-law and chief organizer of Iraq's WMD program, defected to Jordan. He revealed that Iraq was continuing to conceal weapons and missiles and the capacity to build many more.

* Saddam supported terrorism by paying bounties to families of Palestinian suicide bombers, by trying to assassinate former president George H. W. Bush, and by sheltering known terrorists.

* There is no dispute that Saddam was working to build long-range missiles in violation of UN resolutions.

* Even if he did not possess actual WMDs, Saddam's regime had the capability to provide technical know-how to international terrorists on how to build WMDs.

* Liberals didn't object to the U.S. launching a preemptive war in Yugoslavia, even though Yugoslavia posed no threat to the U.S. and its leader, Slobodan Milosevic,

had engaged in nowhere near the violence, murder, and mayhem perpetrated by Saddam. The UN never approved the U.S. war in Yugoslavia and there was never even a suggestion that Milosevic ever possessed or sought WMDs.

★ Going to war for the "wrong" reasons does not necessarily make the war unjust. President Abraham Lincoln fought the U.S. Civil War to "preserve the Union"—not to free the slaves. Yet, we now justify the Civil War because it freed the slaves. Likewise, in Iraq, twenty-six million Iraqis were freed from the tyranny of Saddam.

THE BEST WAY TO GIVE PEACE A CHANCE IN IRAQ: KEEP THE U.S. MILITARY KICKING BUTT

Liberals worry that Iraq is a "quagmire" and "another Vietnam" and insist that we should bring our troops home. But where do you want to fight the front line of the war on terror—in Iraq or in Iowa?

★ ★ ★ ★ ★

Here's what the liberals say. . .

LIBERAL LUNACY:
"The invasion of Iraq is hideously expensive."

Funny how tax-and-spend liberals suddenly become parsimonious cost-cutters when it comes to defending America. But in this post–9/11 era, the costs of our occupation of Iraq can't be looked at with a dollars-and-cents mentality. Whatever it costs to protect our freedoms, it's a bargain.

The real question is: What would the costs be if we left Iraq? The 9/11 attacks probably cost us at least $95 billion. New York City spent almost $5 billion just to clean up Ground Zero. Now, how much more would it cost us if a suicide bomber attacked a nuclear power plant in the

U.S., or if a terrorist used a nuclear device in any major city?

The invasion of Iraq must be regarded as an investment in the Middle East—an opportunity to create a powerful ally where the seeds of democracy can be planted. Ultimately, the money we spend in Iraq will give the U.S. a toehold in the Middle East and help us shape its future. It's already working: Libyan strongman Muammar Gaddafi's recent decision to cooperate fully with the U.S. to ensure that Libya is rid of any weapons of mass destruction is a direct result of our actions in Iraq. How much is that worth, compared to the cost of a Libyan nuke hitting Washington?

LIBERAL LUNACY:
"The occupation will cost too many American lives."

Each time an American gives his or her life on the battlefield it's a tragedy. However, defending the country is a serious and a dangerous endeavor. To protect our nation, American blood must sometimes be spilled and American treasure spent. The Americans who have sacrificed their lives in the war on terror, and those who will, do so for the most honorable of causes. They die to protect our nation and our way of life. It's that simple.

Unlike America's secretaries, accountants, and waiters, our soldiers have the benefit of confronting terrorists with tanks, aircraft carriers, and fighter jets. We're all better off if trained American soldiers are placed in harm's way overseas rather than here in our backyard where average, everyday American civilians would be placed on the front line.

LIBERAL LUNACY:
"The invasion of Iraq does nothing to make the U.S. safer."

As Donald Rumsfeld has said, it's better to fight them in Baghdad than in Boise. Fighting wars in Iraq and Afghanistan takes the fight to our enemies. It also increases our chance of winning. Fighting in the Middle East gives us access to the heart of the war on terror. Iraq has become a magnet for terrorists because of the American presence, and that's great. Let the mercenaries, jihadists, and other nuts spend their time and money racing to Iraq instead of plotting new attacks on American soil. If something has to be blown up in the war on terror, aren't we better off with tents and camels blowing up in the Middle East instead of high-rise office buildings in the U.S.?

Before the U.S. invasions of Afghanistan and Iraq, the front lines in the war on terror were in our backyard. Consider the 1993 World Trade Center bombing, the 9/11 attacks, the planned attacks on the Lincoln Tunnel, the attempts to destroy the Seattle Space Needle during the 2000 millennium celebrations, and Jose Padilla's dirty bomb plan. Now the front lines of the war have shifted from the streets of America to those of Iraq. The Muslim fanatics may still be able to strike here, but there is no doubt that their global operations have been weakened, and shifted away from Western

> ### CONSERVATIVES SAY IT BEST...
>
> Secretary of Defense Donald Rumsfeld reiterated the essential rationale of the war: It is better to fight and capture terrorists in Baghdad than in Baltimore or Boise.

targets. What's wrong with moving the locus of Islamist-generated insanity to the Middle East?

LIBERAL LUNACY:
"The U.S. is acting like a colonial power, and shouldn't be interfering with the sovereignty of another nation."

Regardless, contrary to liberal hysteria, the U.S. is not trying to turn Iraq into an American colony or the fifty-first state. We have a long, successful history of nation-building after wars: Japan, Germany, Panama, and more. In none of those places did we establish colonies, although we could have.

Nervous Middle Eastern dictators, of course, decry America as "imperialist." They're worried that Western ideas of democracy and individual liberty have penetrated so deeply even into their own countries that a successful democratic example in Iraq, combined with the dismal performance of their own political systems, could now overwhelm them. And the liberal American media plays along, taking their "anti-imperialist" claptrap seriously.

BUSH VS. CLINTON

President George W. Bush approved the largest increase in the defense budget since the Reagan administration: 26 percent.[1] Bush's 2005 proposed budget for the Department of Defense is $402 billion, a 7 percent increase from 2004.[2]

In contrast, President Clinton's 2000 budget for the DoD was $262 billion. He wanted to cut defense spending by $10 billion in 2000 in favor of spending on liberal social programs.[3] Clinton squandered America's "peace dividend" and left American security underfunded and vulnerable to attack.

It's a joke even to mention Iraqi sovereignty in the context of Saddam. Saddam was a thug who ruled without the consent of the Iraqi people. Thus, under Saddam, Iraq had no legitimate claim to sovereignty.

LIBERAL LUNACY:
"A democracy can't succeed in Iraq."

If liberal educators and bureaucrats hadn't destroyed the public schools, they might have learned some history. World history shows that democracy is a relatively recent phenomenon. With the exception of the Athenian Greeks, democratic governments did not arise in significant numbers until the late eighteenth century. But since the American Revolution, country after country has adopted republican forms of government. This proves that democracy can work in countries with no democratic tradition. In the last sixty years alone, Germany, Japan, India, Italy, and many Latin American countries have become democratic republics. Why not Iraq?

LIBERAL LUNACY:
"Our troops in Iraq just inflame the local population."

Listen to the liberals long enough, and you might get the idea that the common Iraqi is unhappy without Saddam's oppression. But back on earth, liberating oppressed people from tyrannical police states inflames no one except those who ran the police states. Except for Iraqis who were high-ranking Baathist party officials, what human being, Iraqi or otherwise (except perhaps the Marquis de Sade), would cry out, "Oh, no! Don't take away our oppressor! Don't get rid of the man who can torture, rape, or murder me or my family with the snap of his fingers! How can we go on without him?"

Consider Afghanistan. Before we went to war against the Taliban, the liberals told us the same thing: Our invasion would just inflame the locals. Yeah, those Afghanis looked pretty angry as they cheered the American and British troops entering Kabul. Those women who were once again free to go out of their homes and go to school, they looked enraged. Those folks who could listen to music and fly kites again, they were mad as hell. And of course, there was never any uprising on the "Arab Street."

LIBERAL LUNACY:
"Occupying Iraq will create more terrorists."

They said the same thing about invading Iraq, remember? And they're wrong on both counts. By fighting crime, do we encourage crime? Did killing Nazis create more Nazis? Did attacking the Ku Klux Klan create more KKK members? Heck, did fighting Native Americans create more Native Americans (or just more casinos)? There are now ninety countries engaged in the war on terror. Putting pressure on terrorists' finances, and making it harder for them to travel, recruit, and raise cash does not create more terrorists. Terrorists are created when kids are taught that suicide bombers go to Heaven—not when we hunt them down and kill them, sending them to their just rewards.

VRWC TALKING POINTS

It's better for American soldiers armed with aircraft carrier groups, fighter planes, and helicopters to fight the war on terror in Iraq than for American civilians to fight the war on the streets of Kansas. America's success in Iraq is critical to our national security. Consider:

* It gives the U.S. a toehold in the vital Middle East, where we can better monitor and influence the Arab nations supporting international terrorism.

* History proves without a doubt that democratic nations can be created from non-democratic beginnings. In the twentieth century alone, new democracies arose in Germany, Japan, Italy, India, and many Latin American countries. Why not Iraq now?

* Since the beginning of the invasion of Iraq, about 550 American military personnel have been killed. Though each such death is a tragedy, in World War II, there were 221 combat deaths a day for four years and in Vietnam there were about eighteen American deaths each day. About 109 people a day die each day on America's highways. In 2003, New York City experienced 596 murders and Chicago had 599 murders.

* Liberals apparently understand the meaning of the word "unilateral" about as well as they understood what the meaning of the word "is" is. The U.S. is not acting "unilaterally" in Iraq, for dozens of other nations joined the Coalition of the Willing to liberate the Iraqi people from Saddam's regime.

WHO WOULD
OSAMA VOTE FOR?

The Democrats like to say that Republicans are bungling
the war on terror. But if you were Osama bin Laden, who
would you want in the White House: George W. Bush and
Donald Rumsfeld, or an antiwar, United Nations–loving
Democrat?

★ ★ ★ ★ ★

Here's what the liberals say. . .

LIBERAL LUNACY:
"The Republicans are playing politics
with American lives."

The liberal's main contribution to the war on terror is to
act like a child in the backseat during a cross-country
trip—to just sit, whine, and complain "Are we there yet?"
Back in World War II, Republicans rallied behind a
Democratic president for the good of our nation. But it
apparently doesn't work both ways: In a cynical display of
raw partisan politics, today's Democratic presidential candidates are undermining our national security by resisting
the president at every step of the war on terror—and then

accusing him of politicizing the war. The Democrats are operating on the assumption that they can't support anything positive for the country while a Republican president is in office, because it might benefit the Republicans.

Liberals have dragged their feet in the war on terror from the beginning. From the beginning of the invasion of Afghanistan, they started prattling about there being not enough troops, that the Afghan rebels were poorly trained, and where's Osama? As President Bush tried to defend the country by ridding the world of Saddam Hussein, liberals continued to whine. They tried to bog down the war effort by insisting that we needed UN approval, that we needed the French and Germans on board, that the UN weapons inspectors needed more time, quagmire quagmire, etc., etc.

This is rank hypocrisy. Liberals claim to be morally superior to those Americans who take Militant Islamists at their word when they say they want to destroy the U.S. and the West. Yet they call George Bush a "Nazi" and prattle on about "Bushitler" because he is acting in the manner that will best protect the nation. So I guess it's evil for President Bush to fight evil. Go figure!

LIBERAL LUNACY:
"The use of American military power
is wrong and arrogant."

Some of these guys must have kept their high going since the Summer of Love. Otherwise how could any sane person, even a liberal, believe that it is actually the U.S. that poses the greatest danger to the world today? Liberals really hate the exercise of American power. They believe that military power is inherently evil—unless it is used by

Janet Reno to capture Elian Gonzalez or by communist groups in the name of free health care, housing, and education, just the way their heroes Che Guevara and Fidel Castro did it.

Really, their opposition to the terror war is no surprise; liberals hate the idea of fighting violence with violence. They have repeatedly trumpeted the myth that the best defense against a violent attacker is to give him what he wants. Thanks to this advice, we got policies that on 9/11 led to three jetliners full of people being overtaken by a handful of guys wielding only box cutters. We saw in the fields of Pennsylvania that day what Americans fighting back can accomplish.

In fact, it's hard to use American power for evil. Our system of checks and balances and the give and take of open debate in our country make it virtually impossible. Any use of American military or economic power will be examined publicly within the country. The use of military or economic power is the ultimate expression of a democracy.

LIBERAL LUNACY:
"We should not defend ourselves militarily until a threat is imminent."

The same liberals who want to deny us handguns for personal self-defense, as well as the means to defend ourselves against nuclear missiles, are now telling us that we should not defend ourselves militarily until we are in immediate danger of being attacked. Liberals would wait until the missiles are in the sky (thus making the threat "imminent") before fighting back. So I guess they would prefer to see a nuclear device explode in New York harbor than support an operation dedicated to finding and destroying that device before it is detonated. If America had had a chance to sink the Japanese navy in November 1941, apparently modern-day liberals would have opposed it.

But in an era where weapons can kill millions, we simply can't afford to wait. In insisting that we should, liberals are approaching the war on terrorism from the same fantasyland that gave us midnight basketball as a crime-fighting program and considered the accused rapist Bill Clinton to be the great defender of American women. Liberals seem incapable or unwilling to acknowledge that America is in a war against people who want to destroy us. Liberals want to surrender first and then negotiate; conservatives want to win an unconditional surrender and then negotiate. Just as history has judged Western Europe harshly for its failure to recognize and preempt Nazi aggression in the 1930s, so too will history "judge harshly those who saw this coming danger but failed to act. In the new world we have entered, the only path to peace and security is the path of action."[1] When Hitler's Nazi troops marched into the Rhineland in 1936, the soldiers were told to turn back at any sign of a military response from France or England. At that time, Hitler had the will to destroy us, but not the power. As former Israeli prime minister Benjamin Netanyahu explains, "Today we have the power to destroy them. Now we must summon the will to do so."[2] Let us learn from history.

LIBERAL LUNACY:
"Bush is a foreign policy cowboy just like Ronald Reagan."

All this "cowboy" talk is just European sloganeering. Americans elect politicians to represent their interests and presidents are elected to protect the country from foreign threats. President Bush is doing just that. Anyway, if being a cowboy results in foreign policy successes similar to those brought about by that other "American cowboy," Ronald Reagan, then let's amend the Constitution to mandate the issuance of spurs, a six-shooter, and a ten-gallon hat to every new president. Reagan's aggressive, America-first stance toward the former Soviet Union led to the end of not only the Soviet Union but also of communism as a viable form of political economy (though communism continues in spirit in the halls of academia). Bush has been similarly proactive and aggressive in advancing American interests at the expense of the Militant Islamists. Bush, like Reagan, is right.

Liberals don't seem to understand that peace marches and antiwar demonstrations on New York's Fifth Avenue won't stop terrorism. (If that worked, terrorism would have been forever destroyed by the marches, protest, love-ins, and adolescent tantrums of the 1960s.) Offering bin Laden a Starbucks Frappuccino just won't do the trick. Wars are not won by rhetoric. You must fight it to win it—just ask Neville Chamberlain, who made the mistake of believing that he could negotiate for "peace in our time" with Hitler—only to find England later having to fight a war against a much stronger, better prepared, and fully militarized Germany.

VRWC TALKING POINTS

Why is it that since the Vietnam War, liberals practice nothing but appeasement and defeatism?

★ Jimmy Carter surrendered Afghanistan to the Soviets, turned over the Panama Canal to Panama, and betrayed the Shah of Iran, which allowed Iran to fall into the control of the Ayatollah Khomeini—thus giving Islamofacists an oil-rich nation from which to fund and launch terrorist attacks.

★ Clinton gutted our defense budget to fund liberal domestic programs like midnight basketball, failed to respond seriously to the growing threat from international terrorism, and rejected three different offers to apprehend Osama bin Laden.

★ Even before President Bush's response to 9/11, the Democrats for National Security website notes that voters in the 2000 election preferred George W. Bush on the national security issue by a margin of nearly three to one.[3]

WANT SANITY AND CIVILIZATION IN THE MIDDLE EAST? SUPPORT ISRAEL

So, Israel is to blame for the problems in the Middle East? When was the last time an Israeli Jew blew himself up in a Palestinian pizza parlor?

★ ★ ★ ★ ★

Here's what the liberals say. . .

LIBERAL LUNACY:
"The Palestinians and the Arab Middle East lash out at the West because the U.S. supports Israel."

Maybe for once the liberals are right. The Palestinians and the Arab Middle East probably really do hate us because we support Israel. But so what? They probably also hate us because we are rich and powerful, but this is not exactly an argument to bring back the horse and buggy and kerosene lamps.

We should support Israel because Israel is the only sane country in the region. Why should the U.S. withdraw support for a steadfast ally just because Palestinian schools teach children that Jews don't belong in the Middle East?

We have to keep on supporting Israel, both because doing so is in the best interests of America and because it is the morally right thing to do. Right now there is only one stable Western-style democracy in the Middle East. If we abandon Israel, there may be none.

LIBERAL LUNACY:
"The Jews stole the land of Israel
from the Palestinians."

Do you really think that the struggle between Israel and the Palestinians is about land? Was Hitler's decision to occupy the Rhineland in 1936 only about German control of the Rhineland? If the struggle between the Israelis and Palestinians was really about land in the West Bank, why were the Arabs attacking Israel in 1948, 1956, and 1967, when the entire West Bank was under control of Arab Jordan?

The Arab states, including the Palestinian Authority, want to eliminate Jews from the Middle East (or at least subjugate them under Islamic rule). Author David Horowitz astutely explains that "[a]s the Arab Muslims of the Palestine Mandate and their successors had previously announced through suicide bombings that target Jewish babies; through maps that erase the state of Israel; through the 1999 rejection of a peace plan that included 95 percent of their negotiating demands; through the never-abandoned 1964 liberation manifesto that calls for the obliteration of Israel as the 'Zionist entity;' through their own spiritual leaders, the Grand Muftis of Jerusalem—the one who today calls for the destruction of America and the Jews and the one who yesterday, in the midst of the Nazi Holocaust, was a disciple and ally of Adolf Hitler—

What Muslim textbooks teach:

- "Many [Jews and Christians] lead such decadent and immoral lives that lying, alcohol, nudity, pornography, racism, foul language, premarital sex, homosexuality, and everything else are accepted in the society, churches, and synagogues."[3]

- "Jews subscribe to a belief in racial superiority.... Their religion even teaches them to call down curses upon the worship places of non-Jews whenever they pass by them!"[4]

- "Judaism and Christianity are deviant religions."[5]

- "Befriending the unbelievers, through loving and cooperating with them while knowing that they are unbelievers, makes those who are their friends the same as them."[6]

the real agenda of Arafat and the Palestinian leadership is and has always been the elimination of Jewry from the Middle East."[1]

Stolen land? The land comprising the State of Israel comprises about 1 percent of the land in the Middle East. How much of that 1 percent has oil? Virtually zero.

Nobody cared about this forsaken land before 1948, when the State of Israel was established. But immediately after Israel was founded, the neighboring Arab nations tried to invade and destroy it. Why? Did the Arab forces really just want that spit of oil-less land in the middle of the desert? No. They just couldn't stand the idea of a Jewish state because Jews were—well, Jews.

A sane island in an insane part of the world...

- Although Jews have always lived on the lands of modern-day Israel, the nation of Israel did not come into existence until 1948.

- After World War II, the UN made a decision to partition the area of modern-day Israel and its surroundings between the Jews and Arabs living there. In 1948, the United Nations recognized the State of Israel as a nation.

- The next day, the neighboring Arab states, including Jordan, Egypt, Iraq, Lebanon, and Syria, attacked Israel in an attempt to destroy the newly recognized state. Israel thwarted the military onslaught of its Arab neighbors, in the first of many such instances.

- Israel fought wars with neighboring Arab nations in 1948, 1956, 1967, and 1973.

- Israel has a population of about 6.5 million and is surrounded by twenty-two Arab states containing an Arab population of about 300 million.

Today, if Israel ceded the West Bank to the Palestinians, 80 percent of the Israeli population would be within Palestinian artillery and mortar range. Israel's forward-looking radar that can see into the Arab states would be blind. This would be like giving Osama bin Laden a protected base in Jersey City and then waiting for him to shell Manhattan. Did you ever notice that the Israeli settlements are on the hilltops? It's not because that's where the fertile land is and it's not just for a view of the scenery.

It is the defensive high ground; with the hills in Israeli control, the Palestinians can't shell the valleys below.

Anyway, why should Israel have to return any land to the Arabs? What is this notion about returning land to the loser after a war anyway? Why do you think they're called the Victors and the Vanquished? When you lose a war, why do you think they call it *losing*? I don't remember the U.S. giving back the East Coast to the British, or Florida or the Dakotas to the American Indians. I can't recall that we returned California to Mexico, at least not yet. Just because the U.S. set an example after World War II and returned Japan and Germany to their citizens doesn't mean that this is the automatic outcome of war. The U.S. would never have relinquished Japan and Germany if they would have continued to wage guerilla war against our troops. We would have crushed them. As it was, we only gave up administering these countries after we were absolutely certain that they would do us no more harm in the foreseeable future. In fact, we permanently disarmed Japan; so much so that having no army is now part of its constitution. Why aren't the Israelis entitled to at least the same terms from the Palestinians? Israel has fought and won several wars against the Arabs, so, at this point, Israel has every right to guffaw at requests to return land to the Palestians and Arabs.

LIBERAL LUNACY:

"Even if the Jews deserve their own nation because of the Holocaust, why should the Palestinians have to give up their land for it? They're not responsible for the Holocaust."

The founding of Israel did not displace any Arabs. Remember: There was no Palestinian state on the land of modern-day Israel before 1948. The land of Israel did not belong to any one nation. When the Ottoman Empire fell after World War I, the land was largely empty, except for some stateless Jews and Arabs. The land then technically came under British control. In 1917, Great Britain issued the Balfour Declaration, which said that a Jewish state should be created in the land known as Palestine. Nobody had the idea that this would involve the displacement of a huge native population, because there wasn't one.

In stark contrast to how Jews are treated in Arab countries (they are not recognized as citizens and are not allowed to practice the Jewish religion), Israel's large Arab citizenry (about one million) can practice their religion, vote in elections, and even serve in Israel's legislative body, the Knesset. Arabs living in Arab nations have far fewer political and economic freedoms than Arabs living in Israel.

LIBERAL LUNACY:
"Israelis are responsible for the Palestinian refugee problem."

Actually, the Arab states created the "Palestinian refugee" problem. The so-called "Palestinians" are no different, in ethnicity or language or anything else, from the Arab people in the neighboring Arab countries. But the Arab governments have flatly and repeatedly refused to take in Palestinian refugees. They prefer instead to keep the Palestinians homeless and stateless so that they can use them to complain about Israel.

Did you know that at the time Israel was founded, there were hundreds of thousands of Jews living in the Arab countries of the Middle East? But there has never been a "Jewish refugee" problem in the Middle East. Why? Because in contrast to the Arab nations' self-serving snubbing of the Palestinians, the Israelis accepted 600,000 Jewish refugees from Arab countries into their tiny nation.

LIBERAL LUNACY:
"Israel is the real terrorist state in the Middle East."

Yes, Israel is tough on terrorists and their supporters. Would you prefer that the one sane, Western-style democracy in the Middle East just lie down and die? Israel has no obligation to commit suicide for the convenience of the Palestinians. We know that terrorists simply see a tepid response and often even an invitation to negotiate as a sign of weakness, prompting them to step up attacks. Bill Clinton's weak response to the "Black Hawk Down" incident in Somalia emboldened Osama bin Laden. If Israel eases up on the terrorists, it would only encourage more terrorist attacks.

True, Israel isn't perfect. What country is? In fighting for its existence, and for the lives of its citizens who have been subjected to military and terrorist attacks for over fifty years, Israel has made the occasional mistake. Israeli soldiers have on occasion shot an innocent bystander or killed children by mistake. Did you catch that? *By mistake.*

Palestinian suicide bombers *intentionally* target civilians. On October 4, 2003, it happened yet again: A Palestinian terrorist blew up a bomb in Haifa, Israel, killing twenty-one people, including four children. The Palestinian people's response? Most were thrilled![2] And American lefties hail these suicidal monsters as "freedom fighters." How can the U.S., while fighting the global war against terrorism, support any group where a majority favors deadly terrorist attacks against civilians and children? What could possibly justify blowing up restaurants and pizza parlors full of ordinary people? And, by the way, when was the last time you read about an Israeli blowing himself up in the name of Moses in the middle of a Palestinian marketplace?

But when Israel kills a few civilians in the course of military operations, it is condemned and demonized by the Arab world and the United Nations. There's something wrong with this picture: Civilian deaths are not the goal of Israel's military. But they are the goal of Hamas, Islamic Jihad, the PLO, and the rest of the Arab terrorist groups. These groups should be condemned, not Israel.

It's true that Nobel Peace Prize–dreaming European diplomats constantly browbeat Israeli leaders to make further concessions to the Palestinians and the Arab world in the "name of peace." However, if you were an Israeli Jew, would be willing to trust your life and future to the advice of those kindly, open-minded, French and German humanists? The only thing that might be worse would be to have Jimmy Carter as your chief negotiator. Unfortunately, the Palestinians and Arabs view "peace" as a tactic, rather than a goal to be actually achieved. Interludes between Palestinian campaigns of terror against Israel simply become opportunities for the Palestinians to clean their weapons and rearm. We saw this clearly, after the Oslo Accords, when the Israelis intercepted a ship carrying fifty tons of weapons bound for Palestine in 2002. Yasser Arafat's Palestinian Authority had paid for the weapons. Apparently, just another Nobel Peace Prize winner doing his part for world peace.

Bottom line: Israel is a terrorist state only in the fevered imaginations of Yasser Arafat and Noam Chomsky. Israel is not perfect, but it represents a modern democratic country and a staunch ally of the United States in a region critical to U.S. interests.

VRWC TALKING POINTS

The U.S. should support sanity, rationality, tolerance, individual freedom, and democracy wherever we can around the globe. Unlike its neighbors in the Middle East, Israel is a sane, liberal democracy respectful of the rule of law and religious tolerance. Supporting Israel is both in America's interest and the morally right thing to do.

* The founding of Israel didn't displace any Arabs. The Arab states created the "Palestinian refugee" problem. They refuse to take in the refugees, preferring instead to keep them nameless and stateless so that they can be used against Israel.

* Arabs living in Arab nations have far fewer political and economic freedoms than Arabs living in Israel.

* Israel has an absolute right to use military force to defend itself against Militant Islamic terrorists and the nations that support them.

* Palestinian suicide bombers *intentionally* target civilians. Civilian deaths are never the goals of the Israeli military. But they are the goals of Hamas, Islamic Jihad, the PLO. These groups should be condemned, not Israel.

HELPLESSNESS IS NOT A VIRTUE: WHY WE NEED MISSILE DEFENSE

Liberals think having a defense against nuclear missiles is "provocative" and "dangerous." But what do liberals want us to do if a rogue state launches a nuclear missile at us—duck?

★ ★ ★ ★ ★

Here's what the liberals say. . .

LIBERAL LUNACY:
"America doesn't really need a missile defense system."

You gotta be kidding me. The U.S. is the biggest bullseye on the face of the Earth. Communist China despises us. Rogue states in the former Soviet Union are some of the largest suppliers of weapons and training to terrorist cells throughout the world—and both would love to take a shot at the big guy. North Korea has been unabashed in its pursuit of a nuclear weapons program with the chief purpose of "defending" North Korea from American aggression. Let's not forget about any number of the al Qaeda cells or other terrorist organizations with which we are currently at war that would not hesitate to detonate a nuclear weapon on U.S. soil if given the chance.

Contrary to what over half of Americans think, the U.S. today has no way to intercept and destroy a nuclear missile launched at us.[1] Despite President Reagan's best efforts to commit the U.S. to developing and deploying an anti-ballistic missile defense system, the end of the Cold War and politicians eager to spend the "peace dividend" stalled the deployment of such a system. So what can we do now if the Chinese, North Koreans, or some crazed Islamic state launches a nuclear missile at us? Duck.

LIBERAL LUNACY:
"An anti-ballistic missile system
would be too expensive."

Okay, Hillary, explain it to me: expensive compared to what? How expensive would it be compared to, say, a nuclear attack? The 9/11 attacks not only killed 3,000 people—they also caused billions of dollars in property damage and cost the national economy trillions in lost wealth, added insurance and security costs, and lowered business confidence. A nuclear missile attack could damage the U.S. far more than even 9/11 in terms of casualties as well as economic and psychological devastation. According to the Council on Foreign Relations, the detonation of a nuclear weapon in New York City would likely kill over 800,000 people and injure another 900,000 while producing "radioactive fallout that could kill half the exposed population as far as 10–15 miles away."[2] The need to destroy or deter even a single nuclear missile is obvious.

Do we really want mutually assured destruction?

- In 1972, the U.S. entered into the Anti–Ballistic Missile Defense Treaty, which prohibited the U.S. and the Soviet Union from deploying defense systems that would shield their respective countries from a missile attack by the other.

- This gave rise to the doctrine of mutually assured destruction: that a nuclear attack by either the U.S. or the Soviet Union would ensure the mutual destruction of both nations.

- In 1983, President Ronald Reagan announced that it was immoral for American political leaders to allow their citizens to be held hostage by the Soviet nuclear arsenal. Reagan began developing an anti–ballistic missile system designed to destroy incoming missiles, providing a protective umbrella over the U.S.

- With the collapse of the Soviet Union, some of the urgency for an anti–ballistic missile system faded. Under President Bill Clinton, defense budgets were substantially reduced in order to spend more money on liberal domestic programs.

- Today, the U.S. remains vulnerable to attack from rogue states and terrorists. A single nuclear missile targeted at an urban area could kill a million Americans and cause grave damage to our national and world economy.

LIBERAL LUNACY:
"An anti–ballistic missile system, if it worked at all, wouldn't stop 100 percent of the missiles."

Wrong! Just deploying the system would deter actual attacks and nuclear blackmail. If it stopped just one nuclear missile, the system would pay for itself. Please don't confuse this argument with the liberal bleat used to ban guns and impose hundreds of nanny-state regulations, i.e., "If we just save one life, the new law will be justified." Stopping a nuclear missile from detonating in the U.S. would not save "just one life," but a million.

Also, an anti-ballistic missile system really is technologically feasible. What's wrong with these liberals? Have they forgotten that research and development pay off, and that technology can always be improved? Have they forgotten that where there's a will there's a way? Don't they remember that it was John F. Kennedy, a Democrat, who challenged NASA to find a way to place a man on the moon within a decade, and NASA did so?

For those liberals who took only politically correct classes in Sociology, let's explain the process known as inventing. Okay, here's how this works. We invest money and time and apply lots of brains and computers and, then, lo and behold, we have B-1 bombers, Patriot missiles that work, heat-seeking missiles, bulletproof vests, unmanned drones, and all sorts of smart bombs and weaponry. It can be this way for an anti-ballistic missile system, too. Nobody used medical MRIs or CAT scans a few decades ago. Why not? Because they didn't exist. Now they do.

So what if we had a missile system that doesn't work perfectly? Liberals, remember that the process of invention also includes an element known as trial and error. When inventors try a prototype and it fails, they go back to the drawing board. Unlike liberals who, despite the complete failure of the greatest socialist economy in history (that would be the former Soviet Union) still think that a government-controlled economy can work, military contractors and engineers learn from the mistakes—and go on to build better and more effective weapon and defense systems. The U.S. has put men on the moon, robots on Mars, and (with the help of alpha male Al Gore, of course) helped create the Internet. Surely we can develop a working missile defense system.

> **CONVERSATION STOPPER**
>
> Contrary to what over half of Americans think, the U.S. today has no way to intercept and destroy a nuclear missile launched at us. So what can we do if the Chinese, North Koreans, or some crazed Islamic state launches a nuclear missle at us? Duck.

Anyway, the U.S. is already moving toward the successful deployment of an ABM system. The U.S. just recently conducted yet another successful test: A missile launched from a U.S. Navy Aegis cruiser destroyed a dummy warhead over the Pacific.[3]

LIBERAL LUNACY:
"Because a missile defense system would not prevent terrorists from attacking by sea or some other way, why bother?"

This is an apples and oranges argument. We must defend ourselves against all lethal threats, whatever their source.

Ballistic missile defense is specifically designed to deter one particular kind of attack, and it would do so effectively. That terrorists may strike the U.S. using other weapons of mass destruction "is no reason to leave our country naked to missile attack. Taking the missile threat seriously does not imply that the terrorist threat is somehow unimportant. A homeowner aiming to deter burglars would not take pains to lock the doors and deliberately leave the windows wide open."[4]

LIBERAL LUNACY:
"Rogue states will be deterred by U.S. military strength, making a missile barrier unnecessary."

Please. Let's look at Saddam Hussein. This guy invaded Kuwait. Despite the fact that the entire world (including many Arab states) opposed him, he refused to withdraw voluntarily. Obviously he wasn't deterred by the combined military might of the U.S. and the entire world. Likewise, North Korea was not deterred by American military might when it agreed to and then immediately breached its 1994 Jimmy Carter-engineered agreement not to acquire the enriched uranium necessary for the production of nuclear weapons. Unlike the Soviet Union, which viewed the use of nuclear weapons as a last resort, many rogue states and terrorists groups see weapons of mass destruction "as weapons of choice, not of last resort."[5] Just one more reason why we need a missile shield.

LIBERAL LUNACY:

"Deploying an anti–ballistic missile system would violate the 1972 Anti-Ballistic Missile Treaty between the U.S. and the Soviet Union."

Note to Howard Dean, who recently referred to the Soviet Union four times on Chris Matthews's *Hardball*: There is no more Soviet Union. That's right, I know liberal hearts are broken, but the greatest attempt to make socialism work now lies on the junk heap of history. Since the 1972 ABM Treaty had only two signatories—the U.S. and the Soviet Union—and because one of those has pulled a permanent Houdini disappearing act, any obligation the U.S. had to comply with the ABM Treaty has ended.[6]

VRWC TALKING POINTS

America is the biggest target of rogue states and terrorists. It's only common sense that we need the ability to intercept and destroy nuclear missiles launched at us. Consider:

★ By a two to one margin, the American people want a missile defense system.[7] Why can't liberals agree to defend the country? Isn't that government's primary purpose?

★ A single nuclear detonation in New York City would likely kill over 800,000 people and injure another 900,000 while producing "radioactive fallout that could kill half the exposed population as far as 10–15 miles away," according to the Council on Foreign Relations.

★ We know the threat is real; it's time for our nuclear defense to be real too. We don't need a second Pearl Harbor or 9/11.

AMERICA THE BEAUTIFUL: WHY THIS "ARROGANT, UNILATERAL, RACIST, GUN-CRAZED SOCIETY" IS THE ENVY OF THE WORLD

Only a liberal could think the Pledge of Allegiance violates the U.S. Constitution, or that Americans have a history of nothing but sins against women, minorities, and workers. You gotta ask the liberals a question: If America is so terrible, why are you still here?

★ ★ ★ ★ ★

Here's what the liberals say. . .

LIBERAL LUNACY:
"The U.S. exploited, murdered, and stole the country from Disney's Pocahontas, the Lone Ranger's Tonto, and the rest of the peaceful, environmentally conscious Native Americans (formerly known as Indians)."

True, Americans took much of the land we enjoy today by force of arms. But so what? When people were settling this land, most land disputes were settled by force of arms. The U.S. was formed only after winning the American Revolution against the British. Should we now feel sorry for Tony Blair and the rest of Parliament because we took their land? We also took Texas and much of the Western

United States from the Empire of Spain and Mexico. Should we now send Jimmy Carter to Mexico to give back this land like he gave back the Panama Canal? Remember, the world has been a very bloody place for a long, long time. Most people in the world today occupy land that was conquered and taken from somebody else.

Even the Native Americans got into the act. Long before Columbus sailed the ocean blue in 1492, North American Indians were warring, torturing, and raping one another. Just ask the Chippewas about their impression of

America: it's getting better all the time

As economists Stephen Moore and Julian Simon explained in *It's Getting Better All the Time*:

- The nineteenth century in America was an era of tuberculosis, typhoid, sanitariums, child labor, horse manure, candles, twelve-hour workdays, Jim Crow laws, tenements, slaughterhouses, and outhouses. Lynchings were common back then. If you lived to age fifty, you counted your blessings. "For a mother to have all four of her children live to adulthood was to dramatically beat the odds of nature," according to Moore and Simon. About one in four American children died before the age of fourteen.

- One hundred years ago parents lived in fear of their child's death; these days, "middle-class suburban parents live in fear of their child's not making the county select soccer team."

- In 1901, the average American life expectancy at birth was forty-nine. Today it's seventy-seven.

the Dakotas. Contrary to today's fashionable myth that the American Indians were oppressed, they inflicted plenty of damage on settlers and on each other. Many settlers were killed during Indian raids. (For you Hollywood liberal types, think Daniel Day Lewis in *Last of the Mohicans*.)

I'm sorry, but a few Stone Age people can't claim title to a continent just by waving their hands and saying, "all we can see is ours." But if the Europeans had never come to North America, the Japanese would have been glad to do so in the 1940s. How do you think they would have treated the American Indians? (Think the Rape of Nanking.) Conquest is a constant of human history. Today radical Muslims around the world have declared their intention to transform the world into a unified Islamic state. Would Osama bin Laden take our country from us today if he could? You bet. Thus even today we possess our country not because we have title insurance or a deed registered in some courthouse—but by force of arms. Every day the U.S. depends on its military to stop others from taking our country. If you can't defend your land by force, then you probably won't own it for long.

Am I saying that everything the U.S. did to the American Indians was right? I am not. But we've been using taxpayer monies to subsidize Indian reservations for decades—in essence, reparation payments.

LIBERAL LUNACY:
"The U.S. unnecessarily dropped atomic bombs on the Japanese."

This charge tries to show that the U.S. is morally corrupt and hypocritical. But it doesn't accomplish what liberals want it to. When President Harry Truman, a Democrat, ordered the dropping of the atomic bombs on Japan, the

Germans had already surrendered. But the Japanese hadn't. The Japanese had already sacrificed 3,000 suicide kamikaze bombers to try to destroy the American naval fleet. If the kamikazes had succeeded, an invasion of the Japanese mainland would have been near impossible.

Throughout World War II, the Japanese had fought to the death. On Iwo Jima, 8,000 American soldiers died for every mile of island taken. The estimated loss of life from an American invasion of mainland Japan was hundreds of thousands, if not one million, American lives— plus similar numbers of Japanese. Dropping the bomb to save American lives was wholly appropriate, especially since the Japanese had shown no indication of surrendering anytime soon. Indeed, they showed signs of digging in for a long fight—as revealed by the fact that we found Japanese soldiers hiding in jungles years after the war had ended.

LIBERAL LUNACY:
"The U.S. is arrogant and acts unilaterally."

In fact, Americans are not arrogant—although most Americans are proud of our country and grateful for the blessing of being able to live here. It is true that most Americans (at least those in the red states) believe that the U.S. is the greatest country in the world. That Americans rarely renounce their citizenship, board rafts, and shove off for Cuba or the like, proves the point. People risk slavery, poverty, and even death to reach the U.S. Recognizing this fact, however, doesn't make us arrogant—just aware of history and present-day reality, and of the blessings this nation bestows upon its citizenry.

Nor is the U.S. unilateral. If unilateral means that the U.S. acts in its own best interest to ensure the safety of its citizens, then okay, we're unilateralist. What's wrong with that? What nation doesn't act in its best interests? Liberals think that the U.S. acts unilaterally because they can't stand the thought of being despised by the wine-sipping, Brie-eating Europeans, whose decaying welfare states

> ## CONVERSATION STOPPER
>
> Why is America the greatest country in the world? Just ask those who risk slavery, poverty, and even death to reach the U.S. That Americans don't board rafts and shove off for Cuba proves the point.

they admire so much. But don't worry, liberals: France won't stay mad at us for long. After all, if they stay mad, they won't have anyone to fight their next war for them.

LIBERAL LUNACY:
"The U.S. is a fundamentally racist society."

Racist, eh? Name me another country where people of all races, national origins, and economic backgrounds have formed a harmonious "melting pot." People from nations that had been at war with each other for generations became friends in America. By allowing each individual to pursue his or her own interests, the U.S. raised the idea of the individual above that of the group.

Yes, the U.S. had slavery. We also eliminated it. Americans fought the Civil War and freed the slaves. Americans ran the Underground Railroad. Americans fought against and eliminated the entrenched racism of the Jim Crow South.

Today America provides all of its citizens—black, white, yellow, purple, fuchsia, whatever, as well as male or female or confused—the chance to make it on their own merits and efforts.

Liberals, on the other hand, don't think that people can make it by themselves. Instead, they assume that certain groups are helpless and try to use expensive government do-gooders to spoon-feed them the entire way. But the fact is that the most successful people are those who work hard and make their own way in life, without depending on handouts from others. The U.S. gives people a greater opportunity to make it on their own than has any other country in history. Indeed, "[e]ighty percent of America's millionaires are first-generation rich," as explained by Thomas Stanley and William Danko in *The Millionaire Next Door.*

LIBERAL LUNACY:

"America's capitalist economy corrupts our value system so much that Americans are willing to pay golfer Tiger Woods far more money than we pay to public school teachers who are responsible for educating future generations."

This argument is constantly dragged out to show the "unfairness" of the free market and to support public school funding increases. But actually this argument confuses the concepts of "value" and "scarcity." Why does water, which is essential for all living things, sell for pennies a cup, while the same-sized cup of diamonds, which don't do anything but glimmer, could sell for millions of dollars? (Note to male readers: Don't ask a woman to marry you with a cup of water instead of a diamond ring—it generally doesn't work even with female environmentalists from Vermont.) Because water is far more available, and thus less scarce, than diamonds. Likewise, although teachers are extremely valuable to our future

generations, they aren't exactly scarce. But find me someone who can play golf as well as Tiger Woods, and I'll find
you a quick way to get rich. If, however, golf schools were
turning out Tigers in the quantity that education schools
turn out teachers, it would be a different story.

VRWC TALKING POINTS

No country in history gives the common man more
opportunities or has been more successful at enriching
more people than the United States. This is why people
from around the world are willing to risk their lives to
come to America and we never had to build an iron cur-
tain to keep people in.

* No power has ever been more benign than the United
  States—we don't conquer countries, we rebuild them.
  What other country, after being attacked without
  warning and rallying to victory, restores economic
  prosperity in its foes? What other country, having won
  a total victory, wound up with less territory than it had
  when the war began? The U.S. did all of this after
  World War II by restoring Europe and Asia while also
  giving the Philippines its independence.
* Dropping the bomb saved American lives and was
  wholly appropriate—the Japanese had already sent
  3,000 suicide kamakaze bombers and was ready to fight
  to the death.
* American society is self-reforming. We had slavery but
  abolished it. We denied women the right to vote but
  then gave them suffrage. We had laws segregating the
  races but then eliminated the Jim Crow laws.

THE UNITED NATIONS: LET'S TEAR IT DOWN AND PUT UP A STARBUCKS

Liberals believe the United Nations is a great, humane institution, dedicated to peace and international law. Unfortunately, you don't have to be a humane, peaceful, law-abiding country to be a member of the UN. In fact, most of the UN's membership couldn't care less about peace and human rights. Did you know that Libya recently ran the human rights committee and Syria ran the disarmament committee? It might be funny, if it weren't so frightening.

★ ★ ★ ★ ★

Here's what the liberals say. . .

LIBERAL LUNACY:
"The U.S. has a moral and legal obligation to support the UN."

In the immortal words of *Wayne's World*: "Not!" Nothing should compel the U.S. to act against its national interests. Nothing forces the U.S. to belong to (and support financially) an organization that disregards and subverts American interests. Nowhere does the U.S. Constitution require the U.S. to bind itself to any treaty or international organization. The UN has become a tool for anti-American, anti-democratic tyrannies and third-world kleptocracies. What possible moral imperative could there be for supporting it?

Also, by what justification has the U.S. government—through the UN—gotten into the business of funding socialist wealth redistribution programs? The UN subscribes to the liberal socialist Robin Hood mentality of robbing the "rich" to give to the "poor"—but only a tiny percentage of the money the U.S. taxpayer gives to UN programs actually reaches the people it's supposed to help. It's a waste of money, it helps no one, and it should end.

Sure, it was a good idea: an organization in which the nations of the world could come together to meet and talk about mutual concerns. But today the UN is at best impotent and at worst anti-American, anti-Semitic, and

A failed experiment. . .

- The forerunner of the United Nations was the League of Nations, which ceased its activities after failing to prevent World War II.

- The name "United Nations," coined by President Franklin D. Roosevelt, was first used during World War II, when representatives from twenty-six nations pledged their governments to continue fighting together against the Axis Powers.

- Today, the UN spends more than $10 billion each year and has become a tool for anti-American, anti-democratic tyrannies and third-world kleptocracies.

anti-democratic. Let's face it: The UN is a failed experiment. It gives a forum to some of the most despotic leaders in world history, allowing them to prattle self-righteously about how to establish peace on earth. Once their speeches are finished they call home to order a few more executions. These are the thugs we have a moral obligation to? Tell me another.

Unfortunately, it's unlikely that the UN will be eliminated altogether. So, the United States should give lip service to the UN while simultaneously acting in its own interests.

LIBERAL LUNACY:
"The UN can be effective in promoting peace and human rights."

The UN's fifty-nine-year history proves just the opposite: that the UN is incapable of fostering peace or human rights. The UN by itself is just an organization consisting of member states, none of which are bound to do a thing it tells them to do. It's like a giant international Rotary Club or Chamber of Commerce—no offense to Rotary Clubs or Chambers of Commerce!

The UN has repeatedly failed in its essential mission: to preserve world peace. The wars, genocide, and human rights abuses of the majority of its member states (and the UN's failure to stop them) prove this point.

Who is the world's real guardian of freedom, democracy, tolerance, and peace? You guessed it: the United States. Before the UN ever existed, the U.S. and its allies beat the Nazis, the Fascists, and the Japanese imperialists in World War II. Since the UN's creation, the U.S. has prevented a Soviet invasion of Western Europe, protected South Korea from an invasion by North Korea, and gave the communists a run for their money in Vietnam before the "peace" movement caved-in U.S. resolve. We won the Cold War, ending a brutal and expansionist Soviet regime that murdered millions upon millions of people. But do we get credit for all this at the UN? Not on your life.

LIBERAL LUNACY:
"The U.S. shouldn't have acted in Iraq without UN approval—and always criticizes the UN when we don't get our way."

Liberals love the United Nations because it reminds them of the form of government that they support in the United States: bloated, ineffectual, anti-capitalist, and anti-American. Anyway, when did the U.S. ever object to something the UN did that was not in fact objectionable? We criticized the UN for failing to enforce its own resolutions against Iraq—and we were right. We criticized the UN for repeatedly condemning the sole democratic, tolerant, and free nation in the Middle East: Israel—and we were right. We criticized the UN for failing to condemn known terrorists such as Yasser Arafat and his cronies in the Middle East—right again. And for failing to object to Soviet aggression or massacres—anyone willing to stand up for the UN on that one now? History proves it: The U.S. criticizes the UN when the UN acts in a manner contrary to its charter or to the ideals of freedom, democracy, and world peace. What's wrong with that?

Meanwhile, look at what happened with Iraq. The U.S. played by what are supposed to be the rules of the game. President Bush sought and received United Nations approval—in the form of a unanimous Security Council vote—for a renewed campaign to disarm Saddam. Saddam was already in defiance of a whole catalogue of UN resolutions, giving us more than enough legal justification for going in. But even if the UN had declined to give its initial approval to Bush's policy, Bush

> Liberals love the United Nations because it reminds them of the form of government that they support in the United States: bloated, ineffectual, anti-capitalist, and anti-American.

was hardly acting without precedent when he took us into Iraq over UN objections. After all, President Clinton resorted to force without UN approval on several occasions. Each time, he received the support of Tom Daschle and his fellow Democrats.

LIBERAL LUNACY:
"The U.S. should submit its national interests to the greater good (as defined by the UN)."

As long as there are separate nation-states in the world, the U.S. government will have an obligation to its citizens to uphold the U.S. Constitution and protect our national interests. The U.S. was founded by the people and for the people. The preamble of the U.S. Constitution begins with the words "We the People of the United States," not "We the People of the World" or "We the People Who Admire Kofi Annan."

Liberals, do you really think that the UN and Kofi Annan have our best interests at heart? Do you really think that they will even give us a fair shake? UN bureaucrats aren't elected by the American people and certainly don't represent the American people. Consider some facts: In 2001, the U.S. was voted off the UN Human Rights

Commission. The country in charge of that Commission? That would be the great human rights paragon, Libya. Meanwhile, in charge of the disarmament committee is another great member of the family of nations: Syria.

Still unconvinced? Still ready to make Dubya say "How high?" every time Kofi says "Jump"? Then let's go to the history tapes. The UN has repeatedly failed to prevent genocidal massacres. It sat idly by during the genocides in Cambodia, Rwanda, and the former Yugoslavia. The UN has also failed to prevent wars in Africa, the Balkans, Korea, Vietnam, Afghanistan, and the Middle East. Whatever the causes or merits of these conflicts, they prove that the UN failed to bring peace to the world— and that without U.S. involvement, the UN is a hollow shell.

Not to be entirely negative: The UN does provide its members with a chance to have coffee with delightful people from around the world. That's why we'd be better off tearing the place down and putting up a Starbucks.

VRWC TALKING POINTS

The U.S. should never subvert its national interests to those of the UN. The U.S. represents individual freedom, democracy, free markets, and the rule of law. The UN is full of members whose nations are nothing more than tyrannies, kleptocracies, and criminal enterprises masquerading as countries.

★ Why should the U.S. respect an organization representing the interests of North Korea, Libya, Syria, and China?

★ The UN experiment failed. Though the UN supposedly exists to preserve world peace, it has failed to do so. The UN sat idly by during genocides in Cambodia, Rwanda, and the former Yugoslavia. The UN has failed to broker peace between Israel and the Palestinians and failed to prevent twentieth-century wars in Korea, Vietnam, the Balkans, Afghanistan, and the Middle East.

★ History shows that the U.S., not the UN, is the global force for spreading freedom, prosperity, tolerance, and peace. The UN sat idly by as the U.S. won the Cold War and thwarted aggression by North Korea and the Soviet Union.

★ Liberals love the UN because it reminds them of the form of government that they want to see in America: bloated, ineffectual, anti-capitalist, and anti-American.

GET YOUR LAWS OFF MY POCKETBOOK: WHY LOWER TAXES BENEFIT EVERYONE

Conservatives think that people who earn the money spend it best. Liberals think that the government knows best how to spend that money. Let's compromise and make everyone happy. Let's have high taxes on liberals and low taxes on conservatives!

★ ★ ★ ★ ★

Here's what the liberals say. . .

LIBERAL LUNACY:
"High taxes enable the government to do good and create jobs."

Nope, sorry. Read my lips: the government does not create jobs. Liberals frequently defend government spending by pointing to the visible effects of government spending. Liberal politicians who want to take your money for some alleged "greater good" can point to a government-funded bridge or school and boast about the marvels of governmental works. But they don't tell you about the very real yet invisible costs of such government spending.[1] To build a bridge or a school, the government needs to get money from somewhere. After all, the government has no money of its own. To raise money for government works, the tax collector takes money and wealth from me and you and the rest of the productive private sector. We pay for government projects through our taxes.

And how do taxpayers manage to pay their tax bills? By working. In taking money from taxpayers for programs deemed worthy by some random politician, the government deprives the taxpayers of the fruits of their labors. If they had been allowed to keep their money, they would have spent it and strengthened the economy—which *really* creates jobs. Every dollar the government takes from me is one less dollar I have to spend on a home, a car, or on my family. We can see the bridge or school the government built with our money, but we don't see those invisible people who remain unemployed because (due to my high tax bill) I couldn't buy a new home, a new car, or send my child to private school.

LIBERAL LUNACY:
"We need high taxes in order to provide for the poor."

Why is it right for some government bureaucrat to decide when and how and to what extent I care for the needy? Economist Leonard Read explains: "It is absurd for me forcibly to impose my will upon you: dictate what you are to discover, invent, create, where you shall work, the hours of your labor, the wage you shall receive, what and with whom you shall exchange. And it is just as absurd," he continues, for government "to try to forcibly direct and control your creative or productive or peaceful actions."[2]

What the government is costing you

According to the Americans for Tax Reform Foundation:[3]

- The "Cost of Government Day" is the date in the calendar year when the average American worker has earned enough gross income to pay off his or her share of spending and regulatory burdens imposed by all levels of government.

- In 2003, that day was July 11—4.5 days later than in 2002. This means that Americans must work, "on average, 193 days out of the year just to meet all the costs imposed by government."

- The "cost of government consumes nearly 53 percent of national income."

- The total taxes paid in fiscal year 2001 came out to $1.991 trillion. $994 billion—49.9 percent—came from individual income taxes.

Even when it comes to a good cause like caring for the poor. Not to mention, only a small percentage of the federal budget actually goes to the poor.

Nevertheless, largely in the name of caring for the poor, today the top 5 percent of income earners in the U.S. pay half of the federal income tax. The top 10 percent of income earners pay two-thirds of the federal income tax. The bottom half of American taxpayers pay either nothing or very little in federal income taxes. Thus, the great burden of income tax is imposed on a relatively small percentage of the nation's income earners. Taking a substantial portion of income from those in society who are the most productive is not only unfair, it's harmful to those who are theoretically supposed to benefit from government benevolence.

Who will provide jobs for the unemployed or the poor, other than those who have the financial and intellectual wherewithal to start businesses, create jobs, and, yes, even pay taxes? Remember, you can't be an employee without an employer. As Ronald Reagan explained, there's no better welfare program than getting a job. Letting people keep their money helps everyone. The more money left in the hands of workers, investors, and entrepreneurs—that is, the productive class—the more we all benefit, including the poor. Smaller government and lower taxes create more incentives to work, save, invest, and engage in entre-

Who pays?

- The top 2.7 percent of American income earners pay almost half of the total taxes.

- The top 5 percent of income earners pay half of the federal income tax. The bottom half of American taxpayers pay either nothing or very little in federal income taxes.

- 20.8 percent of Americans paid 85.2 percent of the income taxes received by the federal government in 2002.

- George W. Bush has proposed, fought for, and won a tax cut each and every year of his presidency.

preneurial endeavors. When the government takes less in taxes and regulatory costs, businessmen have more money to hire people. Consumers have more money to spend in those businesses. More people work, and more people prosper. Simple, isn't it?

LIBERAL LUNACY:
"We need high taxes to punish the greedy rich."

Perhaps because so many liberal politicians, such as Ted Kennedy, Howard Dean, and John Kerry, were born into or married wealth, they fail to understand the direct relationship between hard work, saving, and economic success. This one is especially ironic coming from limousine liberals and radical-chic types who ought to be wealthy enough to realize that punishing the rich means punishing everyone. Says a wise and self-made rich man, Rush Limbaugh: "It's easy to talk about punishing wealthy people for their supposed greed. But when you talk about taxing the rich, you're talking about taxing capital. And taxing capital results in damage to more than just the wealthy. In other words, you can't punish the wealthy without also punishing the middle class. That's because the wealthy invest their capital to create new jobs, most of which accrue to those not wealthy."[4]

Government policy shouldn't punish the rich for their success; it should instead empower the non-rich to get rich. Conservatives want to make the poor rich, while liberals want to make the rich poor. Winston Churchill said it best: "The inherent vice of capitalism is the unequal sharing of blessings; the inherent virtue of socialism is the equal sharing of miseries."

Also, where in the name of Joe Stalin did any American ever get the idea that it was the role of our government to punish people for being wealthy— and even to enslave them? Taxation is, after all, a form of slavery. Hyperbolic? Hysterical? I don't think so. What is slavery, anyway? A slave is someone who is owned by another. The slave owner tells the slave what he can and can't do. Most importantly from the slave owner's perspective, the owner gets to keep not just the slave himself but also the fruits of the slave's labor without having to pay a dime for them.

Today, those of us who pay taxes have become partial de facto slaves to the government. If the government decides that you have give up 50 percent of your income regardless of whether you want to, you must do so. The government decides how much of the fruits of your labor it will seize. If you refuse to play along, you go to jail.

That modern government engages in activities that enslave us is not just unfortunate; it's inconsistent with the principles of the individual freedom upon which our nation was founded. You should be allowed to act as you see fit unless doing so would violate the natural rights of another. Says Leonard Read: "Man either accepts the idea that the Creator is the endower of rights, or he submits to the idea that the state is the endower of rights. I can think of no other alternative."[5]

LIBERAL LUNACY:
"We can't afford to cut taxes.
Cutting government jobs will hurt the economy."

Balderdash. If the government needs to balance its budget, it should act like a private company and lay off workers and cut costs. Laying off government workers—few of whom produce anything other than paper and zany regulations—would actually save taxpayers money and thus help the economy. Taxpayers would have more money because they would be paying less to the government.

Anyway, most government workers are parasites who produce nothing but paper and costs to the nation's productive private sector. They just hurt the economy, and with it all our standards of living, by taking money from the productive private sector and sending it to the unproductive government sector. Remember, in order to receive money in the free market private sector, you must provide a service or product for which someone is willing to pay. Thus, in the free market private sector, there is a direct relationship between satisfying people's wants and receiving economic rewards. The private sector is the productive sector because there are economic incentives for providing consumers with goods and services they want. This direct relationship between satisfying human wants and needs, on the one hand, and receiving economic rewards in the form of more money, on the other hand, does not exist in the government sector. Most government employees remain employed not because anyone wants their services, but because their jobs are mandated to exist by virtue of a law enacted by politicians who do not have to actually bear the costs of the law.

VRWC TALKING POINTS

More money in people's pockets is better than more money in bureaucrats' pockets. The people who earn their money have a greater incentive to spend their money wisely than do government workers spending other people's money. Where did the government get the idea that its job was to punish people for being wealthy?

★ Today, the top 5 percent of income earners in the U.S. pay 50 percent of the federal income tax. The top 10 percent pay two-thirds of the federal income tax.

★ Higher taxes = more government = more regulation = more red tape = more bureaucrats and more lawyers. Do we really want more big government, bureaucrats, and lawyers?

★ Americans spend more than half the year—an average of 193 days according to the Americans for Tax Reform Foundation—"just to meet all the costs imposed by government."

★ Businesspeople and the free market give far more to society than do most government bureaucrats. Businesses provide jobs, places to eat, to bank, to live, to buy cars, to shop, to buy gas, to buy medical products, and to buy life-saving, life-enhancing drugs. When you want to buy food, appliances, clothes, holiday gifts, or arrange for a vacation, you don't call the government, you call business.

REAGAN VS. CLINTON: GUESS WHO *REALLY* SAVED THE ECONOMY?

Okay, liberals, this one is easy. If jobs, wealth, and tax revenues are created by business, which president would a businessman prefer: low-tax Ronald Reagan or let's-socialize-health-care Bill Clinton?

★ ★ ★ ★ ★

Here's what the liberals say. . .

LIBERAL LUNACY:
"Reagan's tax cuts benefited the rich and hurt ordinary Americans."

Liberals don't really hate Ronald Reagan because they think his tax cuts hurt the poor. Nor do they want high taxes because they care about the poor. They want taxes high so they can have lots of government money on hand, which they can use to create more Democratic voters—voters who depend upon government jobs and subsidies. Democrats need tax revenues to keep government handouts going. After all, Democrats gain power by being able to dole out political goodies. But these goodies cost money—money that has to come from the taxpayer.

Cut off the flow of that money and you cut off the Democrats' power.[1] That's why Ronald Reagan was Public Enemy Number One for liberals: by cutting taxes, Reagan threatened the parasitic, unproductive class dependent upon taxpayer-funded government largesse. This threatened the Democrats' political sustenance.

In 1981, Reagan persuaded Congress to enact his 25 percent across-the-board tax cut. It worked: after Reagan's tax cuts the economy grew (accounting for inflation) by 31 percent between 1983 and 1989, for an annual economic growth rate of 3.5 percent. In the process, the Reagan economy created almost twenty million new jobs, doubled the value of the stock market, and reduced both poverty and unemployment rates.[2]

LIBERAL LUNACY:
"Reaganomics was bad
for the economy and the nation."

There they go again. Reaganomics wasn't bad for the economy or the nation, but it was bad for liberals. Reagan once explained that "the government's view of the economy can be summed up in a few short phrases: If it moves, tax it. If it keeps moving, regulate it. And if it stops moving, subsidize it." In contrast, Reagan understood that the American people, not bureaucrats, were the driving and creative force of the economy. He pointed out: "You can't control the economy without controlling the people." He didn't want to control the people because the people— not the government—make America great.

Reagan's view was simple: if you tax people less, they have more of an incentive to work harder and produce more. By giving Americans the largest tax cut in history,

Reagan knew that people would be freer and would spend more. This would increase income as well as government tax revenues. Even President John F. Kennedy, a Democrat, knew that. In 1962, he cut the federal income tax rate, explaining, "It is a paradoxical truth that the tax rates are too high today and tax revenues are too low, and the soundest way to raise revenues in the long run is to cut taxes now. The purpose of cutting taxes now is not to incur a budget deficit, but to achieve the more prosperous, expanding economy which can bring a budget surplus."[3]

> **Ronald Reagan:**
>
> ❝You can't control the economy without controlling the people.❞
>
> **John F. Kennedy:**
>
> ❝[T]he soundest way to raise revenues in the long run is to cut taxes now. The purpose of cutting taxes now is...to achieve the more prosperous, expanding economy which can bring a budget surplus.❞

LIBERAL LUNACY:
"Reagan's tax cuts created huge budget deficits, placing U.S. taxpayers $1.5 trillion in debt."

It's true: the U.S. government was $1.5 trillion deeper in debt when Ronald Reagan left office than it was when he became president. This deserves a thoughtful, carefully considered response. Ready? Here it comes: So what?

In the 1980s, we were in the middle of a cold war against an expansionist Soviet Union that had already killed tens of millions of its own citizens in the name of a communist utopia. The Soviets had made it plain again and again that they intended to take over the world. Reagan understood that destroying the Soviet Union would not only save the American way of life but would also pay great economic dividends. By treating the Soviet empire for what it was, an anti–human freedom "evil empire," Reagan embarked on a high-tech arms race that the Soviet Union could neither afford nor sustain. And American children no longer had to fall asleep at night worrying about the nuclear holocaust depicted in the movie *The Day After.*

It's true that if Reagan hadn't spent so much money on defense, our debt would have been smaller, but again, so what? America won the Cold War. The $1.5 trillion deficit was the cost of the Reagan military buildup that led to the Soviet Union's collapse. Was this investment in ending the Cold War worth the money? You bet your life it was. Says Dinesh D'Souza, "That investment yielded a world in which the threat of nuclear war has been greatly diminished. Since the Berlin Wall fell, the U.S. government has saved hundreds of billions of dollars in reduced defense allocations." In purely economic terms, economist Larry Lindsey says, "Reagan's military buildup produced a 'fantastic payoff;' it was the best investment the U.S. government ever made."[4]

Also, liberals have probably forgotten that the deficits weren't Reagan's fault in the first place. He had to contend with an extremely liberal U.S. House of Representatives, led by Democratic speaker Tip O'Neill of John Kerry's Taxachusetts. While Reagan pushed for increases in defense spending to rebuild our military after its demise under President Carter, O'Neill insisted on maintaining or increasing spending on liberal social programs (boy, Tip, that War on Poverty spending sure paid off!). Though

Reagan disagreed with the legitimacy of many of these liberal programs, he understood the first principle of politics: don't let the perfect be the enemy of the good. Accordingly, he begrudgingly went along with the Democrats' liberal social spending in order to increase defense spending—and saved the world from murderous Soviet communism.

LIBERAL LUNACY:
"If you want to see great economic growth, look at what we experienced in the 1990s thanks to Bill Clinton."

Got to hand it to the liberal media. They created the "George H. W. Bush recession" and then turned around and created the "Clinton boom." Throughout Bill Clinton's successful run for the presidency in 1992, the media trumpeted talk of "George Herbert Hoover Bush." The liberal media did this while overlooking a minor fact—the U.S. economy had been growing (and thus not in a recession) for well over a year.

The liberal media kept up a steady drumbeat throughout the 1992 election season: the economy was in the tank. They repeated uncritically Clinton's charge that the economy was in the worst shape since the 1930s. Few knew—or had the opportunity to learn from Dan Rather, Ted Koppel, or Peter Jennings—just how false this was.

Contrary to what most Americans believed, the economy wasn't really in a recession. The recession was over by March 1991. Clinton didn't even announce his White House run until months after the recession had ended.

And the Clinton boom? What really saved Clinton was the Republican Congress elected in November 1994. After that, his chances to punish the business community by raising taxes or socializing health care were gone forever. But what was Clinton's pre-November 1994 economic record? Remember, despite his 1992 campaign promise to cut taxes, he raised taxes by a record $240 billion over five years. Clinton even admitted in 1995, "People in this room are still mad at me at that budget because you think I raised your taxes too much. Well, it might surprise you to know I think I raised them too much, too."

Today, Clinton's former economic advisors try to claim credit for the tech boom of the 1990s. They say it resulted from their targeted tax hikes. (Interesting how Clinton said that he was wrong to raise taxes in 1995, but isn't singing the same tune today.) In fact, the technology boom of the late 1990s took place thanks to millions of entreprenurial, and hardworking Americans who created millions of jobs and economic opportunities.

VRWC TALKING POINTS

If you tax something, you get less of it. If you subsidize it, you get more of it. We should avoid taxing the productive private sector to subsidize the unproductive, bloated government bureaucracy. Consider:

★ President Ronald Reagan lowered taxes and reduced the federal bureaucracy, which unleashed the power of the American people. The result? Twenty million new jobs, low unemployment, technological innovation, and rising standards of living.

★ President Bill Clinton got elected after the economy had already been growing for a year, and then proceeded to raise taxes and attempt to socialize one-seventh of the economy (i.e., health care).

★ Clinton's economic liberalism was sharply rebuked by the American people in the mid-term elections of 1994. With the election of a Republican Congress, the economy could breathe a sigh of relief, confident that the Republicans would thwart any zany liberal economic proposals. The result? The 1990s economic boom!

THE RUNAWAY JUDICIARY: RULE OF LAW, NOT RULE BY JUDGES

Liberals are always for "the people"—in theory, that is. In fact, they increasingly prefer to enact their agenda through the courts, because "the people" won't vote for their candidates or policies. But, who should make the laws—the American people and their elected representatives, or unelected judges and jurors?

* * * * *

Here's what the liberals say. . .

LIBERAL LUNACY:
"Tort law helps the little guy against companies that place profit over people and consumer safety."

This argument fails to recognize the fundamental truth that, in terms of in our litigation-happy society, most of us are "companies." Whether we run the companies as management, work at the companies as employees, work for companies that are our customers, buy from companies as consumers, or hold company stocks and bonds for retirement, virtually every one of us is dependent upon business in one way or another. American companies are you, me, and even our liberal friends—who hit up private companies for donations to Greenpeace and siphon off taxes to pay for zany social programs.

Of course, a company seeks to make a profit. That's its whole point for existing. If, however, it tries to make a profit by making slipshod or dangerous products, you don't need to get a lawyer to make things right. The marketplace will make the company pay in lost sales and bad publicity. A company has no incentive to kill or hurt its customers. Remember: no government regulation was needed to remove the Edsel from Ford's production line. Likewise, companies now use safety as a selling point: Check out the ad campaigns for every liberal's favorite set of wheels, the Volvo, or every liberal's favorite whipping boy, the SUV.

LIBERAL LUNACY:
"We need tort law to punish doctors and businesses that are negligent."

Conservatives don't want to abolish the tort system. Certainly people and companies that hurt people, intentionally or unintentionally, should pay a price. A system designed to hold individuals and companies accountable for their wrongdoing is different from a system in which defendants can be financially destroyed by the mere cost of being sued or by a runaway jury.

Because of our litigious culture, juries have immense power but little accountability. Should it be this way? Should a randomly selected set of eight unelected, unaccountable jurors in a single town in a single state have the lawful power to effectively ban products and destroy industries that produce products and services that the rest of the nation would like to buy?

Let's say a company spends tens of millions of dollars researching, inventing, and testing a new drug to cure a life-threatening disease. After shepherding the drug through an approval process that takes many years with the U.S. Food and Drug Administration, the drug is approved and sold to the public. Ten years pass as the drug amasses a reputation as a real life-saver. But then, two plain-

> **CONVERSATION STOPPER**
>
> Liberals run to the courts to get from friendly judges what they can't get from the democratic process.

tiffs sue the company, claiming that its scientists failed to identify a dangerous side effect of the drug. At the trial, a jury (none of whom are scientists and none of whom attended college) decides that the company's scientists made serious mistakes. It awards the plaintiffs $3 million in compensatory damages and $50 million in punitive damages. This verdict bankrupts the company. The life-saving drug is taken off the market.

Is America better off? Thanks to runaway lawsuits, helpful drugs, valuable products, and useful tools are pulled from the shelves.

In the same vein, negligence cases have become the newest form of the lottery. Litigants know they can win millions with the right case—and potential defendants know it too. In personal negligence cases, the average award was almost $3 million in 1999.[1] A restaurant in Seattle now requires diners to sign a liability waiver before they can be served a fried banana ice cream dessert. Before enjoying the dessert, diners must promise not to bring an "obesity-related lawsuit" against the restaurant.[2]

But the costs are huge as well: In April 2002, the Council of Economic Advisors found that even by using a conservative cost figure of $180 billion for the direct cost of the U.S. tort system, the "excessive" portion (not allocated to compensating victims for their losses and not allocated for the administration costs of transferring money from the liable defendant to wronged plaintiff) of the tort tax is the "equivalent to a 2 percent tax on consumption, a 3 percent tax on wages, or a 5 percent tax on capital income. As with any tax, the economic burden of the 'tort tax' is ultimately borne by individuals through higher prices, reduced wages, or decreased investment returns."[3]

In 2001, the cost of American tort litigation was $205 billion. That's $721 for every person in America. Know what this cost was in 1950? 87 bucks (adjusted for inflation).[4]

LIBERAL LUNACY:
"We need activist courts to protect the American people from themselves."

Justice? Is that what you call it? Liberals always run to the courts to get from friendly judges what they can't get from the democratic process. When California's Proposition 187, designed to deny taxpayer money in the form of social services and welfare from going to illegal aliens, was passed by 60 percent of California voters in November 1994, a federal court immediately stopped the law from taking effect. To this day, it hasn't been substantially implemented. Similarly, in November 1996, California voters passed the California Civil Rights Initiative: Proposition 209. This outlawed race and gender preferences in public education, employment, and contracting. But again judges thwarted the popular will. A federal district court initially prevented the law from going into effect and, to this day, aspects of the law are still being litigated in the courts.

The most extreme example of liberals using the judiciary to force the people to accept their will is the case of Mr. Almost President, Al Gore. After he lost the initial count and the automatic recount in Florida, he sued to overturn the election results that kept going against him. And just recently, when Congress enacted the federal "Do Not Call" law prohibiting telemarketers from calling registered citizens, one federal court kept the statute from taking effect because the FCC supposedly lacked the authority to enforce the law. Then, when Congress subsequently gave the FCC clear authority to enforce the law, yet another federal court prohibited the law from being put in effect. Why? It supposedly violated the First Amendment right of telemarketers! (Finally, a federal appellate court stepped in and has allowed the law to take effect.)

Liberal judges have interpreted the Supreme Court's authority to "interpret the law" as meaning that they can make the law. In their own defense, these judges explain that they're simply interpreting the "living Constitution," keeping the document "current" with the "changing times." Actually, the Framers of the Constitution contemplated the need for constitutional change by permitting amendments under Article V. True, it is not always easy to obtain the virtual consensus of society needed to amend the Constitution. So liberals have taken to the guise of this "living Constitution" idea to advance their agenda

---

Sign Here Before You Take a Bite:

A Seattle restaurant now requires diners to sign a liability waiver before they can be served a fried banana ice cream dessert. Diners must promise not to bring an "obesity-related lawsuit" against the restaurant.

The tort jackpot

- Studies place the cost of America's tort system at over $200 billion annually. That's over 2 percent of U.S. gross domestic product. The cost of tort claims has grown four times faster than the U.S. economy since 1930.[5]

- Most of the tort system's costs don't go to victims at all: Awards to injured plaintiffs amount to just 46 cents of every dollar spent on tort litigation. The other 54 cents goes to lawyers and insurance companies.[6]

- In 1999, the average jury verdict award was $1,004,308—240 percent higher than in 1994, when it was $418,478. A growing number of awards (14 percent) were in excess of $1 million. In vehicle accident cases, the average award during this recent five-year period climbed from $75,127 to $315,653, while in personal negligence cases, the average award skyrocketed from $264,765 to $2,959,047.[7]

without the minor inconvenience of submitting their proposals to a vote.

There are countless important social issues that should have been resolved by the democratic process instead of by unelected judges. The most notorious example of this is the 1973 *Roe v. Wade* decision, in which the Supreme Court struck down laws prohibiting abortion on the grounds of an imagined Constitutional "right to privacy." Where exactly is the "right to the privacy" in the Constitution—or the "right to abortion," for that matter?

Read the document! You won't find either one. You'll find the words "keep and bear arms" and "property," but not "privacy" or "abortion."

But a liberal activist Supreme Court won't be stopped, even when its decisions contradict the Constitution's explicit words. In 1972, the Court struck down (temporarily, as it eventually turned out) the death penalty— despite the clear reference to the permissibility of the death penalty in the Fifth Amendment to the Constitution.

And most recently, four judges on the Massachusetts supreme court tossed aside the state's three-hundred-year-old definition of marriage as a legal union between man and a woman as being "irrational." That's right, in a single decision, four judges were able to eliminate the three-hundred-year-old law regardless of what any of the other 6.5 million Massachusetts residents thought about the divisive political issue of gay marriage. Even as recently as the 2002–2003 Supreme Court term, the U.S. Supreme Court struck down a Texas law outlawing same-sex sodomy. Once again, this was a decision that should have been left to Texans through the democratic process. Instead, a decision with immense repercussions for our society was decided by nine unelected judges in Washington, D.C.

VRWC TALKING POINTS

The U.S. is suffering from a litigation explosion; far too many people are trying to hit it rich with the nation's tort lottery. The number of lawsuits, as well as their costs and the size of jury verdicts, keeps rising. Conservatives don't want to abolish the tort system—we want a system to hold individuals and companies accountable, not one in which defendants can be destroyed by the mere costs of being sued or by a runaway jury. Consider:

★ The cost of tort litigation was $721 for every person in America. In 1950, it was only 87 bucks.[8]

★ Do we want to live in a society paralyzed by the fear of getting financially destroyed in a lawsuit? Do we want to live in a society so paranoid about getting sued that lawnmowers warn that their rotating blades can cut hands, coffee cups warn that contents are hot, handguns warn that they can kill, clothes irons warn not to iron clothes while they're being worn, and car sun screens (that stretch across parked car windshields to prevent seats from overheating) warn "Do not drive with sun-shield in place"?[9]

★ The average jury award in 1999 of $104,308 was 240 percent higher than in 1994.

★ According to the Council of Economic Advisors, the portion of America's tort tax not attributable to compensating victims or administration costs is the "equivalent to a 2 percent tax on consumption [or] a 3 percent tax on wages."[10]

★ Runaway lawsuits have made malpractice premiums for obstetricians as high as $200,000 a year, or nearly as high as their average salaries.[11]

★ Unelected and unaccountable liberal activist judges do not just interpret the law made by the people's elected representatives; they are making the law by "legislating from the bench."

BIG GOVERNMENT: THANKS, HILLARY, BUT NO THANKS

If a large, intrusive government overregulating human behavior is so great, then why is South Korea more prosperous than North Korea (where millions starved to death in the 1990s), why was West Germany more prosperous than East Germany, why is Taiwan more prosperous than China, and why is the U.S. still thriving while the Soviet Union lies on the trash heap of history?

★ ★ ★ ★ ★

Here's what the liberals say. . .

LIBERAL LUNACY:
"We need big government to protect us against big business."

Hillary Clinton once said that she "would trust big government over big business anytime." But with all due respect to the Woman Who Would Rather Be President Than Right, that's nuts. Why? Because even America's largest companies don't have anything like the power over citizens that the government exercises routinely. Nothing forces you to buy Microsoft software or a General Motors car. Indeed, there have been plenty of extremely successful and supposedly "powerful" companies who within a few years found themselves to be quite mortal. Remember toy maker FAO Schwartz? Retailer Montgomery Ward? Atari? Digital Equipment? But government doesn't go out of business. Nor is it subject to the automatic quality control of the free market. As President Reagan once said, government is like a baby: "It is an alimentary canal with an appetite at one end and no sense of responsibility at the other."

Thanks, Hillary, but I'll take big business over big government anytime.

LIBERAL LUNACY:
"Government must regulate the economy, because free markets create unemployment."

In a certain sense, it's true. Free market economies commit "creative destruction"[1]: They eliminate old industries and jobs but, in the process, create new industries and jobs. By creating new industries and laborsaving technologies, the creative destruction of capitalism creates a better world for everyone. At the start of the twentieth century, about 25 percent of Americans worked in agriculture. Now, only about one in two hundred workers is employed in the agricultural sector. There used to be 1.4 million people working on the railroads. Now there are about 200,000. There used to be 400 manufacturers of automobiles; now there are only a handful. IBM was once considered the great American computer company, but in 1993, IBM almost went bust.

Are these disasters? Hardly. Whenever one industry is destroyed, a new industry is born. Those workers displaced in one industry are now available to work elsewhere in the economy. Certainly the advent of the automobile destroyed lots of jobs in the buggy whip factories, but the rise of the car helped the entire society become more mobile—while simultaneously creating thousands of new jobs making and servicing cars. Liberals fail to understand that an essential (and desirable) part of any capitalist economy is the destruction of jobs—manufacturing jobs in particular. But at the same time, laborsaving devices create more and better jobs while also raising standards of living.

Want full employment in America right now? Ban the use of tractors. How many jobs have been lost in farming over the last 100–150 years due to the advent of the tractor? However, if these farming jobs had not been destroyed by tractors, then food today would not be as cheap and plentiful—and many of us who now toil in air-conditioned office buildings fighting with copy machines would find ourselves sweating in the hot sun harvesting crops. We'd all have jobs, but should we really opt for full employment under such circumstances?

Of course, the recognized societal benefits from free markets do come with a cost. Those who lose their jobs in old, dying industries obviously suffer. However, they too benefit from the cheaper and more plentiful products made available by the new advances that eliminated their jobs. And, they can seek new employment in the new industries that have been created in the process.

LIBERAL LUNACY:
"We need government to compensate for the growing gap between the haves and the have-nots."

Free markets, by harnessing the individual initiative and

intelligence of millions of people, cause an upward march in the quality of life and standard of living for everyone. The technological innovations in particular promote material equality better than any other vehicle. Dinesh D'Souza explains: "A hundred years ago, the rich man drove a car and the poor man walked. That was a big difference. Today, the rich man drives a new Porsche and the poor man drives a second-hand Honda Civic. That is not such a big difference. A century ago, rich families avoided the cold weather by going to Florida for the winter. Meanwhile, poor families braved the elements. Today, most families, whatever their economic status, enjoy central heating; but the poor have benefited more from this invention because it has alleviated a situation from which they previously had no escape."[2]

> ## CONSERVATIVES SAY IT BEST...
>
> " A hundred years ago, the rich man drove a car and the poor man walked. That was a big difference. Today, the rich man drives a new Porsche and the poor man drives a second-hand Honda Civic. That is not such a big difference. "
>
> —Dinesh D'Souza

The free market of ideas and technology, not the government, is closing the gap between the rich and the poor. According to a recent study: "Today the typical American, defined as poor by the government, has a refrigerator, a stove, a clothes washer, a car, air conditioning, a VCR, a microwave, a stereo, and a color TV. He is able to obtain medical care and his home is in good repair and is not over-crowded. By his own report, his family is not hungry and in the last year he had sufficient funds to meet his essential needs. While this individual's life is not opulent, it is equally far from the popular images of poverty conveyed by politicians, the press, and activists."[3] In fact, "[t]he principal nutrition-related problem facing the poor in America is obesity, not hunger; the poor have a higher rate of obesity than other socioeconomic groups.... Nearly 40 percent of the households defined as poor by the U.S. government actually own their own homes" and "poor" Americans have "more housing space and are less likely to be overcrowded than the average citizen in Western Europe."[4]

LIBERAL LUNACY:
"Political freedom is more important than economic freedom. Since we can vote, who cares if government makes rules about zoning, property taxes, and protecting the disabled?"

Let me ask you this: how many Americans (most of whom don't vote anyway) would gladly give up their right to vote if by doing so they'd be excused from paying taxes? There might not be any voters left. And why? Because economic freedom is far more tangible in and important to the daily lives of most Americans than is political freedom—and most Americans just want to be left alone to live their lives as they see fit. Yet liberals want to use government to tell us how to live, what we can pay employees, the types of homes we can live in, and how much of our money we can keep. That ain't freedom, and if Americans could get free from it all by giving up their right to vote, many would jump at the chance.

Economic freedom is political freedom. George Soros is donating over $10 million to defeat President Bush in the 2004 elections. How much of this political freedom

Not tall tales

Stories of wasteful government spending and egregious mismanagement are so numerous as to have become cliché.

- A 2001 report prepared by U.S. senator Fred Thompson (R-TN) finds that the federal government alone wastes taxpayer money due to fraud, waste, and mismanagement to the tune of about $35 billion a year.[6]

- The federal government budgeted $2.6 billion to build Boston's Central Artery (known as the "Big Dig"). But already, the cost of completion is about $14.6 billion—a 560 percent increase.

- The U.S. Department of Interior cannot account for $3 billion it was suppose to be holding for American Indians.

- NASA lost all four of its spacecraft bound for Mars in 1999 in part because its staff failed to convert feet to meters.

- Medicare paid millions of dollars to beneficiaries whom it knew to be dead.

- The IRS admits that it has no idea how much it collects in Social Security and Medicare taxes (But watch out, it will come auditing if you don't have all your receipts in order.)

would he have left if the government taxed away all his wealth? It is important to understand that "[t]o be controlled in our economic pursuits means to be controlled in everything."[5] Though liberals like to emphasize the right to vote (or perhaps the right to an abortion) as the most important freedom in a demo-cracy, an equally important right is the right to be free to earn a living. Though getting a job, earning an income, buying food, buying clothes, going to a restaurant, owning property, renting or buying a home may seem a bit pedestrian to many modern-day political and philosophical theorists, in reality, these are the most important human freedoms. A society that has the power to deny you the right to engage in these basic, daily economic activities has the power to enslave you. While the right to vote for elected officials is important (even Saddam Hussein held elections, as did the Soviets), the right to go about our daily lives is more so.

A moral, just, and successful society recognizes and provides for the protection of individual freedom. In fact, history shows that societies that protect economic freedom also allow human liberty to flourish. Says a 1923 U.S. Supreme Court decision: "Without doubt [liberty] denotes not merely freedom from bodily restraint but also the right of the individual to contract, to engage in any of the common occupations in life, to acquire useful knowledge, to marry, establish a home, and bring up children, to worship God according to the dictates of his own conscience, and generally to enjoy those privileges long recognized at common law as essential to the orderly pursuit of happiness by free men."[7]

Big government is the enemy of these fundamental human freedoms. This country was founded to protect the freedom to choose how to live without meddlesome interference from others. Free people make their own decisions about how to live, how to keep the fruits of their labor, and even how to suffer the ill effects of their decisions. A society that protects these opportunities is moral. Once someone else (even if in the form of a benevolent government bureaucrat) gets to make decisions for you, you become as a child and get treated as such. They get to tell you where to work, how much to charge for your labor, and what you have to do to stay healthy. You lose your self-reliance, your freedom, and the incentives to make wise personal choices and the opportunity to learn from the "school of hard knocks." The worst scenarios are reflected by the former Soviet Union and modern day North Korea, where citizens are denied their freedom to engage in economic transactions—and die as a result of it.

LIBERAL LUNACY:
"Unlike the private sector, the government is motivated by public interest."

Hardly! Businesses give far more to society than do most government projects. Businesses provide us with jobs, places to eat, live, and shop, and even life-saving drugs. Businesses do not get their customers the same way the government does. People go to the government because there's nowhere else to get a driver's license, mail a letter, or get a building permit. People frequent business establishments *voluntarily* and only because those businesses have something they *want*. Bill Gates is rich today because his innovative ideas and products have put computing powers into more hands for less money.

Liberals howl at the "selfish" motivations of economically successful people because they fail to see the tremendous benefits society receives from the efforts of these "selfish" people. Our lives today have been hugely improved over the last decade thanks to the entrepreneurs who through hard work and creative thinking provided us with technology such as computers, cell phones, and DVDs.

And let's talk about the self-anointed "selfless, public-interest oriented" liberals. Remember when Bill Clinton took tax deductions for donating his used underwear? Remember when Al Gore, as a Tennessee landlord, threatened to evict a tenant who complained that her home's plumbing wasn't working? And what about those "selfless" public school teachers unions who never seek pay raises or try to thwart school choice initiatives? And, of course, I suppose that the American Federation of Government Employees, as the largest federal employee labor union, just exists to advance the public interest—not the interests of their members?

VRWC TALKING POINTS

If everyone in America woke up tomorrow and decided they wanted to work for the government, they could not. Why? Because there would be no one to pay the salaries. Without a private sector to create wealth, goods, and services, the government cannot do anything. A thriving private sector is essential to the well-being of the public sector.

★ It's just plain wrong for Hillary to take *your* money for *her* pet projects.

★ Investors, entrepreneurs, and businesses create real jobs; Hillary's government spending creates more government dependents sucking at the teat of big government.

★ Today, the government involves itself in whom we marry (blood tests); whom we work for (licensing); what we eat (irradiated food regulations), where we live (rent control and zoning laws), what we buy (Microsoft and other antitrust cases), how much of our income we get to keep (income taxes), how we travel (auto airbag and mileage regulations), and even our means to defend ourselves and our loved ones (gun control). So much for the land of the free.

★ Compare the United States to the Soviet Union, West Germany to East Germany, the U.S. economy under Jimmy Carter and Ronald Reagan, or today's American economy with that of the European Union. In every case, free markets produce more economic growth, more jobs and higher standards of living than those systems burdened by the heavy hand of government.

DEATH BY A THOUSAND PAPER CUTS: HOW GOVERNMENT REGULATIONS ARE KILLING YOU

Liberals think people can't run their own lives. They say we need government regulations to do that for us. But do we really need regulations requiring Braille keypads on drive-through ATMs?

★ ★ ★ ★ ★

Here's what the liberals say. . .

LIBERAL LUNACY:
"We need government regulations for our own safety."

Yeah, right. We need government regulations to fine barbers for having "too much hair on the floor." To prevent the late Mother Theresa from building a homeless shelter in New York. To require banks to install Braille keypads on drive-through ATMs. To punish farmers for shooting bears in self-defense. To fine casket salesmen for selling their wares without an embalmer's license.

America's unelected royal elite, government bureaucrats, are running amok and declaring war on ordinary Americans and their businesses. It's time to call a halt. Want to do something that is not regulated by the government?

Forget it. Government regulations apply to housing, banking, recreational activities, land use, occupations, and even using the toilet. That's right: Under a 1992 federal law, toilets installed in American homes must be limited to 1.6 gallons per flush; showerheads must limit water usage to 2.5 gallons per minute. I say let's fire the government toilet inspectors and use the money to beef up a few anti-terrorism units—or give it back to the taxpayer. These niggling regulations not only limit our freedoms, they don't even accomplish what they're supposed to.

After all, half of all violations of Occupational Safety and Health Administration (OSHA) regulations don't come from real threats to health and safety, but—horror of horrors—from failure to maintain proper paperwork![1] Call the file cabinet police! OSHA employs over 2,300 people; its 1,000 inspectors visited work sites 36,000 times in 2001 alone, discovering almost 80,000 safety violations. These resulted in fines of $82 million.[2] Feel safer yet? Not so fast: One recent study shows that "increased safety regulation actually increases the occupational death rate."[3] Another estimates that the current regulatory system is actually responsible for as many as 60,000 deaths every year.[4]

Hard to believe? It shouldn't be. Billions of dollars are squandered on eliminating negligible or nonexistent risks, while you remain unprotected from other, more serious ones.

Take the Corporate Average Fuel Economy (CAFE) standards for cars. The direct result of federal fuel economy laws was the manufacture of smaller, more fuel-efficient cars. There was just one catch: These nifty new gas-efficient beauties were much more likely to get flattened in an accident than the old gas-guzzlers. The former head of the National Highway Traffic Safety Administration, Jerry Ralph Curry, reports, "since CAFE legislation took effect, more people have been killed because of it than died in Vietnam."[5] Maybe the liberals should turn their "no blood for oil" slogan on the federal bureaucrats who run their beloved regulatory agencies.

LIBERAL LUNACY:
"We need government regulations to protect small businesses."

Without government regulations, say the liberals, pretty soon Wal-Mart and Staples will run the last mom-and-pop store out of business, and Mom and Pop will be eating watery soup with plastic spoons down at the homeless shelter. But in fact, regulations saddle small businesses with imposing costs and mountains of red tape—so much that it all amounts to a serious threat to the survival of small- and medium-sized businesses, which create two out of every three new jobs in the U.S.[6] The Small Business Administration estimates that small businesses have to pay $5,000 for each employee every year just to keep up with the ridiculous rules and mountains of paperwork that the government requires.[7]

If employers were freed from all these regulations, they could make more money, pay their employees more, or expand their businesses. But as it is, small businesses are strangled by red tape.

LIBERAL LUNACY:
"We need regulation to rein in shady businesses and discourage scofflaws."

Liberals seem to think that if they create minute regulations covering every aspect of business and life, outlaws will turn in their guns and peace will reign in the land. Nobody will be bilked or defrauded, nobody will be conned by hucksters. But these volumes and volumes of legal codes don't really make us any more honest. In fact, regulations are just another form of taxation. They're just another way for the government to exercise control over us.

In 1998, the total cost to the economy of all regulation was estimated to be $700 billion. This is a hidden tax of more than $6,800 per year per American family and equal to about 43 percent of the entire federal spending budget.[8] Today, the costs of the federal regulatory burden has been estimated at over $750 to $860 billion a year, or almost "$10,000 for every American household. Add in state and local regulatory costs, and the burden leaps to $20,000 per household."[9]

The rules are so many and so minute that they're turning us into a nation of criminals. The documents upon

Regulation mania!

- The Code of Federal Regulations is about 75,000 pages long. It takes up twenty feet of bookshelf space—and that doesn't include state and local regulations.

- In less than two years, federal regulatory agencies issued almost 7,000 final rules.

- Federal law even has something to say about your toilet: Toilets installed in American homes must be limited to 1.6 gallons per flush and showerheads must limit water usage to 2.5 gallons per minute.

which this country was founded—the Constitution, Bill of Rights, and Declaration of Independence—are all short and to the point. In stark contrast, the Code of Federal Regulations is about 75,000 pages long. It takes up twenty feet of bookshelf space—and that doesn't include statutes or state and local regulations. The U.S. General Accounting Office (GAO) says that between April 1, 1996, and December 31, 1997, federal regulatory agencies issued almost 7,000 final rules.[10]

Meanwhile, there are about sixty federal regulatory agencies, which exist only to enforce these laws. The sheer volume of regulations makes the law virtually unknowable. These regulations are often so ambiguous and complicated that you need an army of lawyers just to tell you what they mean. All in all, it makes for a situation in which you are most likely, at this very moment, somehow breaking the law.

The most shameful example of this is the tax code. Tax laws are so complex and unreadable that businessmen and families order their financial affairs only with great difficulty and cost. Many must take on the additional expense of hiring professional tax preparers. Every year, Americans spend over 4.6 billion hours at a cost of $140 billion just to comply with the federal tax code and regulations.[11] The result is fewer success stories and fewer businesses in general. When laws are unpredictable, people are less willing to take risks because they can't predict the likely outcomes of their actions.

You want honesty? Deregulate. In 1997, the White House Office of Management and Budget (OMB) admitted that higher prices and inefficient operations are the direct result of stifling regulations. Regulations even discourage entrepreneurs from starting new businesses.

It's time to let a businessman make an honest buck without making him jump through a dizzying array of government hoops. When government relaxes control, Americans prosper. The proof is out there: Over the past twenty years, Americans have reaped the benefits of the deregulation of the transportation, natural gas, and other industries. Experience shows that the profit motive is the best basis for decision-making: The decision maker faces the consequences of his own making. Regulators have no such discipline.

VRWC TALKING POINTS

Regulations do more harm than good because they are made by unaccountable, unelected bureaucrats. Consider:

* Regulations cost our economy about $800 billion each year; a cost of $10,000 to each American household.
* The U.S. Constitution, Bill of Rights, and Declaration of Independence combined add up to about twenty pages. The Code of Federal Regulations is about 75,000 pages long and takes up twenty feet of bookshelf space.
* Regulations cost small business, which create two out of three jobs in America, $5,000 each year for every one of their employees.
* A Harvard University study finds that regulations led to the deaths of 60,000 people each year.
* More people have been killed by the federal government's Corporate Average Fuel Economy (CAFE) standards than "died in Vietnam" according to Jerry Ralph Curry, former head of the National Highway Traffic Safety Administration.

AN "EXIT STRATEGY" FOR THE WAR ON POVERTY: END WELFARE IN AMERICA

Liberals don't seem to understand that if you want to eradicate poverty, you have to know how wealth is created. It doesn't come from government. It doesn't come from sitting on your hands. It comes from getting a job. The liberal architects of our welfare system seem never to have asked the question: Would you work if you were paid not to work?

★ ★ ★ ★ ★

Here's what the liberals say. . .

LIBERAL LUNACY:
"We need welfare to give the poor a safety net."

The American welfare system was originally designed to help the deserving poor with the basic necessities of life: food and shelter. This is honorable, but the current system strays far from these ideals. Now it caters to untold numbers who use welfare as a hammock. Such a deal! Why would you work if you got paid not to work? As an unemployed teenager, why should you wait to have children until you can afford to care for them when the government will pay you a subsidy right now if you have a child?

It's pretty simple: if you tax something, you get less of it; if you subsidize something, you'll get more of it.

Despite decades of research by liberal social workers, psychologists, sociologists, and other assorted do-gooder liberals—and despite $8 trillion in social service spending—has anyone really been able to come up with a better or more successful social program than just going out and getting a job?

Look, sometimes bad things do happen to good people. Some welfare is necessary, although it would be better handled by private charities that can better monitor the effects

Where is the "Exit Strategy"?

- In 1965, when Lyndon Johnson launched the War on Poverty, welfare spending was only $8.9 billion.

- In 2000, total federal and state spending on welfare programs was $434 billion.

- On average, the annual cost of the welfare system today amounts to around $5,600 in taxes from each household.

- As a percentage of gross domestic product, welfare spending has grown from 1.2 percent in 1965 to 4.4 percent today.

- The cost of the War on Poverty has been more than twice the price tag for defeating Germany and Japan in World War II (after adjusting for inflation).

- The amount taxpayers now spend on welfare each year (adjusted for inflation) is greater than the value of the entire U.S. gross national product at the beginning of the twentieth century.[5]

of their own efforts than by the government, which just sends a check. It should be available in limited circumstances to help formerly productive, responsible members of society get back on their feet. Welfare should not, however, be permitted to replace work, marriage, or personal responsibility.

That's because this safety net just doesn't work. Thanks in large part to the perverse financial incentives created by generous welfare programs, illegitimacy, welfare rolls, and crime rates have exploded. Since the rise of government welfare, the American family has disintegrated. Since the 1960s, the number of single-parent households and the number of illegitimate children has gone through the roof. According to the Centers for Disease Control, National Health Statistics, Division of Vital Statistics, when the war on poverty began, only 7.7 percent of American were born out of wedlock—in 2002, that figure was 34.5 percent.[1] Why? Liberal social welfare programs reward illegitimacy, unemployment, and single parenthood. And when you reward such behavior, you get more of it. It's that simple.

LIBERAL LUNACY:
"Conservatives oppose welfare because they're mean and not compassionate toward the poor."

Oh, really? Well, let me tell you something: Conservatives are more compassionate than liberals. Liberals love to talk the talk when it comes to compassion, but they don't walk the walk. Liberals constantly talk about how society should spend more of someone else's money to help out poor children in inner-city schools, but they continually refuse to try school vouchers, which would give inner-city parents the financial ability to remove their children from failing schools and place them in schools that work.

Liberals talk about how Americans should be compassionate to the criminals who commit heinous crimes, but they themselves show little compassion to the victims of crime. Nor do they take any notice of the devastating effects crime has on crime-ridden neighborhoods.

Liberals claim to be compassionate to the poor, but simultaneously overtax the people who give the poor their best chance at a middle-class lifestyle: businessmen and employers who could provide those poor people with jobs.

Conservatives are far more compassionate—and a whole lot less patronizing—than liberals. Liberals think it's "compassionate" to raise taxes on hardworking, productive Americans in order to transfer other people's money to Democratic constituents: welfare recipients and government bureaucrats.

In stark contrast, conservatives show real compassion by trying to create an equal playing field with as many economic opportunities as possible. Making it possible for poor and low-income workers to become self-reliant is far more compassionate—and far more effective—than creating opportunities to receive government handouts.

LIBERAL LUNACY:
"We have welfare to bring fairness
to American economic life."

I don't know what causes it. Maybe they failed to advance beyond their freshman course in Marxism. But for whatever reason, liberals endlessly natter on about how the rich get richer and the poor get poorer, and that it's not fair that some people can fly first class while others can't afford cars. What liberals don't acknowledge is the many years of hard work and sacrifice that are usually needed to create a rich person.

Why is it unfair for a rich person to make lots of money? Imagine if a young woman, Noelle, gets rich after working forty hours a week to pay for college—and studying another forty hours each week. Now imagine if this young lady went to high school with Jack, a guy who decided not to go to college or to get a decent job, and who never did anything to develop any marketable skills. Ten years later, Jack is lucky to find work sweeping up at McDonald's. Noelle has a Park Avenue penthouse. Is that unfair? Not on your life. Noelle's own work and self-sacrifice made her wealthy.

But how would a liberal view this scenario? Predictably. A liberal would immediately label Noelle a member of the "fortunate few," and conclude that she should be punished for her high income by being made to pay high taxes for social welfare programs—which go to benefit poor old Jack. At the ballot box, liberals can count on Jack for political support, because, obviously, Jack is happy to get a piece of Noelle's income. Conservatives look at this same situation and understand that Noelle gets paid more not because she is lucky or because the system doesn't work, but because it does: Her skills and personal qualities (determination, perseverance) paid off in the marketplace. Nothing unfair about that.

LIBERAL LUNACY:
"Without welfare, life below the poverty line would be intolerable."

Come on. This is America—not Bangladesh! As economist Stephen Moore explained in 2000: "Most Americans who are considered 'poor' today have routine access to a quality of housing, food, health care, consumer products, entertainment, communications, and transportation that even the Vanderbilts, the Carnegies, the Rockefellers, and the nineteenth-century European princes, with all their wealth, could not have afforded."[2]

Robert Rector and Sarah Youssef of the Heritage Foundation clarify our terms: "To most Americans, 'poverty' means destitution: an inability to provide a family with nutritious food, appropriate clothing, and reasonable shelter. In reality, only a small fraction of persons classified as 'poor' by the Census Bureau meet this description. The bulk of the 'poor' live in material conditions which would have been judged comfortable or well-off just a few generations ago. Most 'poor' Americans today are better housed, better fed, and own more personal property than average Americans throughout much of this century."[3]

VRWC TALKING POINTS

The "War on Poverty" subsidized poverty and illegitimacy—and guess what? We got more of both. Why? Because if you tax something you get less of it; if you subsidize something, you'll get more of it.

* When the War on Poverty began, only 7.7 percent of American were born out of wedlock—in 2002, that figure was 34.5 percent.[4]

* We've spent $8 trillion in social services, and it hasn't improved on dad's advice: "Go out and get a job."

* We now spend ten times as much on welfare as was spent when Lyndon Johnson launched the War on Poverty. The War on Poverty is LBJ's domestic Vietnam—yet we don't hear the liberals squawking about "what's our exit strategy" in the War on Poverty.

ROUND UP THE USUAL SUSPECTS: WHY TERRORIST PROFILING MAKES SENSE[1]

For liberals, we should *all* be treated as terror suspects—otherwise we're violating civil rights. But if you're looking for terrorists, why harass the Pennsylvania Amish?

★ ★ ★ ★ ★

Here's what the liberals say. . .

LIBERAL LUNACY:
"Law enforcement should not be allowed to consider race at all."

Okay, why not? Law enforcement should be allowed to consider race, ethnicity, sex, or anything else that can rationally be used to identify and thwart terrorists. Surely liberals would agree that liberal icon and then–U.S. Attorney General Robert F. Kennedy acted appropriately in the 1960s when he considered only whites as possible suspects in cases involving the Ku Klux Klan's terrorizing of Southern blacks?[2] Or do liberals believe that RFK should have investigated blacks as vigorously as whites while trying to stop the Klan? In the same way, law enforcement today would be wise to look for Islamic terrorists not among white-haired Norwegian grandmothers, but among those who are most likely to be engaging in terrorism: young Muslim males. Let's take a look at the facts:

- Islamic fundamentalists blew up the U.S. Marine barracks in Beirut in 1983, killing 243 Marines;[3]
- Islamic fundamentalists hijacked the *Achille Lauro* cruise ship and murdered an elderly wheelchair-bound American;[4]
- Islamic fundamentalists murdered 270 innocent people in 1988 by bombing Pan Am flight 103;[5]
- Islamic fundamentalists bombed the World Trade Center in 1993;[6]
- Islamic fundamentalists bombed the U.S. military barracks in Saudi Arabia in 1995, killing 292 people;[7]
- Islamic fundamentalists bombed the American embassies in Kenya and Tanzania in 1997, killing 243 people and injuring over 5,000;[8]
- Islamic fundamentalists bombed the USS Cole in 2000, killing seventeen sailors;[9]
- And on September 11, 2001, Islamic fundamentalists hijacked four airliners and killed 3,000 people.

Should our nation's law enforcement officers be asked to ignore these undeniable facts about the identity of the attackers? Is it really a wise use of our scarce anti-terrorism resources for airport security officers to spend just as much time searching and questioning little old ladies instead of young men of Middle Eastern appearance who just happen to be praying to Allah in the airport lounge? Is it really wrong for security officers to consider the fact that no one but Islamic fanatics have declared any intention to wage war against the United States? Graham Allison, a professor at the Kennedy School of Government at Harvard University, says that it is "more likely than not" that terrorists will seek to detonate a nuclear bomb in New York City.[10] In light of this, should we really ignore any known facts about those seeking our annihilation?

The consideration of race or ethnicity is hardly new in terrorist or criminal profiling.[11] To thwart the Italian mafia, law enforcement investigated Italian males. To stop a Jamaican drug posse, look for Jamaicans. And to stop the Irish Republican Army, find the white guys with brogues. In each of these examples, race and ethnicity are critically important. However, none of them really constitute "racial" profiling. Instead, these examples reflect "criminal" or "terrorist" profiling.

Terrorist profiling can save lives. In 1999, U.S. government officials were "on the lookout for Middle Eastern men when they stopped Ahmed Ressam, an Algerian." In his car, Ressam had bomb-making materials that prosecutors later alleged were intended for an attack on an American airport.[12] While looking for Ressam, should they

If the profile fits. . .

- All twenty-two people on the FBI's most wanted terrorist list are Muslims and virtually all are Arab.

- In June 2003, the Justice Department issued guidelines saying that federal law enforcement efforts may consider race and ethnicity in investigating past acts of terrorism as well as thwarting new ones.

> ## CONSERVATIVES SAY IT BEST...
>
> " 100 percent of successful terrorist attacks on commercial airlines for twenty years have been committed by Arabs. When there is a 100 percent chance, it ceases to be a profile. It's called a 'description of the suspect.' "
>
> —Ann Coulter

have stopped blonde-haired, blue-eyed women too, in the name of fairness?

In debating terrorist profiling, you must be prepared to answer charges that your position is racist. This is a tried-and-true tactic of the Left: They define issues where the liberal position is weak as "taboo," heaping shame on those who dare to challenge them instead of dealing with the substance of the issue. Don't let liberals distort the truth. To defend terrorist profiling is not to suggest that race alone justifies investigating somebody for a crime. Suggesting that someone is guilty of something solely because of race is immoral, wrong, and should be outlawed.[13] Nothing justifies a highway patrolman searching specifically for minority drivers to stop and harass them when there is no reason for suspicion. But that's a far cry from an airport security guard deciding to search the bearded guy in a turban with a Saudi passport, clutching the Qur'an, instead of the Japanese tourist behind him in line.

LIBERAL LUNACY:
"Racial profiling does not work because profiles can change."

Profiles may indeed change. But that just means that the profiling used by law enforcement needs to change as well. In the current war on terrorism, profiles may change, but right now it's pretty clear who the terrorists are. On September 11, 2001, nineteen male Arab fundamentalist Muslims murdered 3,000 people on American soil. They weren't Pennsylvania Dutch Amish, Bible Belt Baptists, or Polish Roman Catholics. Nor are Methodists or Lutherans operating global terrorist networks bent on destroying the United States. Only one religious group is doing that. If the Amish start killing people in the name of their religion, then change the profile. Until then, let's focus on reality.

LIBERAL LUNACY:
"Profiling unfairly scapegoats all Muslims."

Obviously, as President Bush has repeatedly emphasized, the fact that the U.S. is at war with many Islamic fundamentalists doesn't mean that U.S. officials suspect all Muslims of terrorism. But as Michael Kinsley, a well-known liberal commentator, aptly explains: "Today we're at war with a terror network that just killed [3,000] innocents and has anonymous agents in our country planning more slaughter. Are we really supposed to ignore the one identifiable fact that we know about them? That may be asking too much." Terrorist profiling simply recognizes that it is logical to look at certain individuals within the American Muslim community in order to win the current war on terrorism. Non-jihadist Muslims should welcome and cooperate with such efforts, because their lives are at stake too.

VRWC TALKING POINTS

The U.S. should use every legitimate means available to protect ourselves against terrorism, including recognizing the fact that Islamic fundamentalists of Arab descent have perpetrated numerous terrorist attacks against the U.S., including the 9/11 attacks.

★ Liberal Democrat Robert F. Kennedy, while serving as U.S. Attorney General in the 1960s, considered the "race" of members of the Ku Klux Klan as he tried to stop the KKK from terrorizing Southern blacks. Should we learn from Bobby Kennedy?

★ According to Clinton advisor Dick Morris, President Clinton failed to crack down on terrorist-supporting Muslim charities "because of a fear that it would be seen as 'profiling' Islamic charities."

I HAVE A DREAM: LET'S END RACIAL PREFERENCES ONCE AND FOR ALL

Somehow liberals think it's a person's color, not his competence, that should matter. So ask a liberal: Would you be willing to fly on Affirmative Action Airlines or have surgery at Affirmative Action Hospital?

★ ★ ★ ★ ★

Here's what the liberals say. . .

LIBERAL LUNACY:
"We need affirmative action because America is still a racist society."

You gotta be kidding me. How can you say America is still racist? Where are the racists in positions of influence in American society? Just asserting the existence of so-called "institutional racism" is a canard. Prove it! Companies and the government bend over backwards trying to hire and promote qualified minorities. Minorities succeed in all walks of life. If America were racist, its favorite athletes would not be Tiger Woods and Michael Jordan; its favorite entertainers would not be Oprah Winfrey, Bill Cosby, or

> ## CONVERSATION STOPPER
>
> America a racist country? Our favorite athletes are Tiger Woods and Michael Jordan; our favorite entertainers are Oprah Winfrey, Bill Cosby, and Jennifer Lopez; and our nation's leaders? They include Colin Powell and Condoleezza Rice.

Jennifer Lopez; and Colin Powell and Condoleezza Rice wouldn't be helping to lead the nation.

Americans abhor race discrimination. Institutions such as slavery and the government-endorsed policies of "separate but equal" have no support today in the United States. Even the mere use of a racially insensitive slur would cause opprobrium in polite circles. America's racist past is largely that: in the past. Americans cheer wildly for successful minorities on the athletic fields, in entertainment, and in politics.

Claiming that minorities need affirmative action to succeed won't eliminate any residual racism. In fact, it will encourage more racism. Racism's premise is that members of some races are superior to members of other races. Who is implying that all races are not equal today? Not conservatives. Liberals are the ones fostering the notion today that racial minorities are inferior to whites— because liberals claim that minorities need the helping hand of government to succeed, which only whites can succeed without. You know what that is, folks? It's racism. And the liberals are up to their necks in it.

The question posed by the current affirmative action debate is whether race discrimination in favor of racial minorities is appropriate. Conservatives answer this question with an unequivocal "no." The liberal answer: "Sure, if we can buy minority votes by giving minorities special preferences in the guise of justice and righting old wrongs." In reality, racial discrimination is always wrong. It doesn't matter who is doing the discriminating, or if it is being done for a good cause. It's still wrong.

LIBERAL LUNACY:

"We need affirmative action because minorities still lag behind whites in all statistical measurements of the good life (i.e., college degrees, members of white-collar professions, annual income)."

Results aren't guaranteed in America. The Constitution guarantees each of us the freedom to pursue our visions of happiness; it doesn't promise us happiness. Nor does it guarantee that you will succeed, just the opportunity. If I tried out for the Boston Red Sox tomorrow, I know I wouldn't make the team—and race would have nothing to do with it. It isn't society's job to decide the "proper percentage" of whites in medicine or the "proper percentage" of blacks in the NBA. Blacks, women, and others can and do achieve in all aspects of American life without the "helping hand" of big government.

Frederick Douglass, a nineteenth-century African-American abolitionist leader, once told a group of abolitionists: "In regard to the colored people...Do nothing with us! Your doing with us has already played the mischief with us...And if the Negro cannot stand on his own legs, let him fall also. All I ask is, give him a chance to stand on his own legs! Let him alone.... Your interference is doing him positive injury."[1] Today's liberals should take note.

As is usually the case with liberal do-gooder programs, affirmative action harms its intended beneficiaries.

Qualified minorities who succeed because of their own abilities and hard work are frequently tainted in the eyes of others; they can be perceived as having succeeded through affirmative action, not through their own talents.

LIBERAL LUNACY:
"The presence of racial minorities creates 'diversity.'"

Liberals constantly confuse their idea of "diversity" with real diversity. For liberals, it's all about race. They think diversity exists when you have a roomful of people of different skin colors—even if everyone in the room votes Democrat, graduated from an Ivy League school, and writes editorials for the *New York Times*.

In reality, diversity doesn't arise from skin color, but from background and experience. A roomful of racial minorities all agreeing that Karl Marx was a genius and that Ronald Reagan had nothing to do with winning the Cold War is not diverse. However, a room full of individuals of whatever skin color, debating the merits of different intellectual, philosophical, or political viewpoints is real diversity. But that's not the diversity that liberals want.

LIBERAL LUNACY:
"When they oppose affirmative action, conservatives oppose civil rights."

Contrary to liberals' understanding, civil rights isn't about propping up people who are actually incapable of performing the job they've been given. Civil rights should be about leveling the playing field and treating everyone equally under the law—not preferring some over others because of race. Lady Justice is blindfolded for a reason. If she starts to peek out to see the skin color or wealth of a party appearing before her, then justice is no longer blind—and cases are no longer judged on their merits. That's not justice.

Americans willingly accept meritocracies in professional athletics. African-Americans make up a disproportionate number of professional basketball players. Imagine the outcry if affirmative action wonks started requiring NBA teams to carry a quota of white players! But why should meritocracies be acceptable in professional athletics but not in medical school applications? Isn't it more important to have meritocracy when selecting a cardiac surgeon than choosing a pro basketball player? When you're settling down under the cardiologist's knife, what would comfort you more: knowing that he or she was a member of a minority group, or knowing that he or she really earned that degree?

Not convinced, liberals? Then would you be willing to fly as a passenger on Affirmative Action Airlines? "Welcome! At this wonderful new airline, minorities can qualify as pilots by passing a series of tests much easier than those white pilots must take. We've done this to ensure that a socially desirable percentage of our pilots are minorities. Step on board!"

Related to liberals' claim that support for affirmative action is support for civil rights is their contention that affirmative action fulfills the vision of Martin Luther King, Jr. But in fact, Dr. King wanted to create a society where individuals would be judged "not by the color of their skin but by the content of their character." Dr. King dreamed of a "color-blind society" where race would be irrelevant in society and government policy. That's hardly the society that affirmative action creates today.

In fact, Dr. King wanted to see equality of opportunity in America. Affirmative action doesn't attempt to create equality of opportunity, but equality of results. But this is as impossible as it is polarizing. Current affirmative action policies represent the trashing of King's vision. They care only about the color of one's skin, not the content of one's character. Supreme Court Justice Clarence Thomas explained it in sharp terms: "Government-sponsored racial discrimination based on benign prejudice is just as noxious as discrimination inspired by malicious prejudice. In each instance, it is racial discrimination, plain and simple."[2]

VRWC TALKING POINTS

Claiming that minorities need affirmative action to succeed won't eliminate residual racism. It will only encourage more racism. As with most liberal do-gooder programs, racial preferences hurt those they are supposed to help.

★ Race discrimination is wrong—period.

★ Martin Luther King dreamed of a "color-blind society" where race would be irrelevant. Racial preferences are anathema to Dr. King's dream.

★ The Constitution guarantees us the freedom to pursue our visions of happiness; it doesn't promise that we will all achieve success.

★ Admitting less-qualified applicants into any job, program, or school to ensure only skin-deep aesthetic diversity is unfair both to the person denied entry because of race and to the person admitted because of race. The rejected applicant loses the opportunity. The admitted applicant's future accomplishments may be tainted by the perception that his successes arose from racial preferences.

MELTING POT *SÍ*, MULTICULTURALISM NO: BRINGING SANITY TO THE IMMIGRATION ISSUE

Liberals like immigration not because it's good for America, but because they want immigrants to change awful, oppressive America into a multicultural, balkanized country where they can play ethnic politics. But the late U.S. congressman Sonny Bono had it right: "My position on illegal immigration? It's illegal."

★ ★ ★ ★ ★

Here's what the liberals say. . .

LIBERAL LUNACY:
"Multiculturalism and diversity are good for our society."

Is that so? So we should emphasize our differences over our similarities? We should encourage immigrants to embrace the culture of the place they abandoned and reject the culture of the place to which they ran? Great idea! Maybe we'll end up like one of those places where ethnic and cultural differences matter more than anything else—say, Northern Ireland or Bosnia, or maybe Rwanda or India. Gee, I can't wait!

Let's face it: Multiculturalism is dangerous to our nation. Even Bill Clinton saw this: "Ethnic pride," he noted, "is a very good thing. America is one of the places which most reveres the distinctive ethnic, racial, religious heritage of our various peoples. The days when immigrants felt compelled to Anglicize their last name or deny their heritage are, thankfully, gone. But pride in one's ethnic and racial heritage must never become an excuse to withdraw from the larger American community. That does not honor diversity; it breeds divisiveness. And that could weaken America."

Clinton must have been having one of those "New Democrat" days because he even weighed in favor of having immigrants learn English: "Now, it's all very well for someone to say, every one of them should learn English immediately. But we don't at this time necessarily have people who are trained to teach them English in all those languages. So I say to you, it is important for children to retain their native language. But unless they also learn English, they will never reach their full potential in the United States."

I may never utter these words again, but here goes nothing: Bill Clinton was right. Immigrants should acclimate themselves to American culture—not vice versa. If they want to come to the U.S., then they have to speak English. We don't want a balkanized America split into warring ethnic or racial groups. We should impress on Americans that there is a unique American identity, which is inseparable from the American way of freedom and democracy.

Eliminate bilingual education programs. They burden taxpayers while encouraging foreign-language speaking immigrants to refuse to learn English. How does it help immigrants in New York, Chicago, or Los Angeles to give them a chance to speak Farsi, Greek or Spanish—but no incentive to learn English? Forget what's best for the U.S.; how does this help the immigrant get ahead? When an immigrant comes to the U.S., he should be encouraged to

> The Census Bureau estimated that the illegal alien population in 2000 was 8,705,421.

become a true American, not a hyphenated American. He should learn English and understand the value of hard work, self-sufficiency, and independence—not the value of dependence on government programs paid for by the American taxpayer.

LIBERAL LUNACY:
"Illegal immigrants do jobs that Americans don't want to do."

Actually, the more accurate statement is: "Illegal immigrants do jobs that Americans don't want to do at the current wage rates." But so what? Without illegal immigrants would fruit and vegetables be rotting in fields? Would there be no nannies for toddlers in yuppie families or anyone to launder towels in hotels? I doubt it. Simply put, illegal immigrants are not essential to our economy. If there were a decrease in cheap, illegal immigrant labor, employers would simply have to substitute higher-priced domestic employees, legal immigrants, or perhaps greater mechanization.

Still, it's true: To deport illegal aliens would cause disruption. But not for very long. Employers would make the necessary adjustments. Many tasks would be mechanized. But, you say, machines can't replace human labor?

Well, today we build cars with robots and we've even put robots on Mars. Why couldn't we use mechanization to harvest crops? Professor George J. Boras, an economics professor at Harvard University, points to states like Iowa where foreign-born residents are relatively few, yet there are plenty of Americans working in hotels, fast-food restaurants, and other jobs elsewhere held by illegal immigrants.[1]

Indeed, although liberal journalists living on Manhattan's Upper West Side may blanch at the prospect of not having illegal immigrants to clean the tables at their French bistros, or to watch the children while Dad goes to work for the *Village Voice* and Mom for Planned

---

Americans want secure borders

The *Washington Times* reports:

- A Gallup poll from June [2003] found only 13 percent of Americans thought immigration should be increased, while 47 percent said it should be reduced, and 37 percent said it should be kept at its present level.

- A Zogby poll from 2002 found that 58 percent of Americans wanted to reduce immigration, 65 percent disagreed with amnesty, and 68 percent felt the United States should deploy military troops to the border to curb illegal immigration. Meanwhile, 60 percent of Americans believe present immigration levels are a "critical threat to the vital interests of the United States."[2]

Parenthood, the reality is that they could just pay a little more to hire legal help.

LIBERAL LUNACY:
"We should welcome illegal immigrants with a blanket amnesty."

Liberals say that we should just give up and declare victory in our current struggles with illegal immigration by legalizing the current group of illegal immigrants. But previous attempts at amnesty have failed—and led only to more illegal immigration. The principle is simple enough even for a liberal to grasp: If you tax it, you get less; if you reward it, you get more. By granting amnesty to lawbreakers (i.e., illegal aliens), then you encourage more illegal immigration. We tried this in 1986. Congress legalized over three million then–illegal aliens in an attempt to end illegal immigration once and for all. Since then there has been an explosion of illegal immigration.

In any case, illegal immigrants should not be rewarded for breaking the law. Nor should people who entered the U.S. illegally be allowed to gain citizenship before those who arrived legally and followed the rules.

LIBERAL LUNACY:
"How we can justify turning our backs on the world's poorest people?"

I am not going to apologize for saying that our elected officials need to worry about America first. Every other country puts its own interests first; why should America be different? If we accepted every immigrant who wanted to move here, there would be hundreds of millions of foreigners here tomorrow—causing untold problems for our national security and economy. Wouldn't it be better to have a system in which we receive, review and process immigration applications in an orderly manner?

Conservatives should support legal immigration, but not illegal immigration. There is no constitutional or other right for foreigners to immigrate to the U.S.; nevertheless, the U.S. should embrace immigration when doing so advances our national interests. We already have the most generous immigration policy in the world and accept more legal immigrants than other countries. The U.S. admits roughly 800,000 legal immigrants each year who are eligible to become citizens. This is more than all nations in Western Europe combined and more than at any point in American history.[3]

> ## CONSERVATIVES SAY IT BEST...
>
> ❝ My position on illegal immigration? It's illegal. ❞
>
> —The late congressman Sonny Bono

Those who are ready and able to work should be welcomed. Immigration has always benefited a country's economy and strength. However, we should choose carefully. We don't want immigrants who will cost taxpayers more than they bring to the table. If an immigrant thinks he is going to get social services paid for by the tax dollars of hardworking Americans, send him home. We don't need to be the welfare system or soup kitchen to the world.

More important, 9/11 has shown that immigration is also a national security issue. At least fifteen of the nineteen hijackers were in America on that fateful day even though they should have been denied visas—if immigration officials had processed their applications properly.[4]

According to the Census Bureau, in 2000, 114,818 Middle Eastern men and women were estimated to be in the U.S. illegally. Will any of these people ever perpetrate another terrorist attack on American soil? Are you willing to bet that none of them ever will? We already know that about "80,000 illegal criminal aliens, including convicted murderers, rapists, drug dealers, and child molesters who served prison time are loose on the streets of America."[5]

The Beltway sniper, Lee Malvo, and his mother were illegal immigrants from Jamaica. They were arrested in Bellingham, Washington, in 2001. The arresting officers noted in writing that Malvo and his mother should be imprisoned until deportation charges were resolved. This did not happen. Instead, Malvo, despite being caught as an illegal alien, was released without bond and on his recognizance. Shortly after his release, Malvo, with the help of his partner, John Muhammad, went a killing spree that not only killed ten and injured three but also caused public panic. What's the use of spending tax dollars to capture illegal aliens if we're only going to release them back onto the streets? Illegal aliens who are captured should be deported. For the sake of our safety, we need stricter immigration enforcement and control.

VRWC TALKING POINTS

Illegal immigrants should not be rewarded for breaking the law. Those who enter the U.S. illegally should not be allowed to stay.

* Every nation has the right to control its own borders.
* Poll after poll shows that Americans want to secure the nation's borders.
* Immigrants who contribute to our economy are welcome; immigrants who come for welfare are not.
* The U.S. already has a generous immigration policy— admitting more legal immigrants each year than at any point in American history, and more than all the nations in Western Europe combined.
* It is in the interest of every immigrant to become culturally an American—that's why they came here; there's no room for hyphenated Americans.

FORMER FETUSES, UNITE: WHY BEING PRO-LIFE IS THE RIGHT CHOICE

Why are liberals willing to stay up all night outside a prison singing John Lennon's "Imagine" while awaiting the execution of a man who raped, tortured, and murdered a young girl, but then fight ferociously for the right to execute an unborn child?

★ ★ ★ ★ ★

Here's what the liberals say. . .

LIBERAL LUNACY:
"The fetus is not a human life."

"Life begins," said Democratic presidential candidate Wesley Clark, "with the mother's decision." So I guess infanticide is just fine if that's what Mom wants?

In reality, a "human being" is a living member of the species *Homo sapiens*. Leaving aside the self-serving political posturing, objective science can determine without a reasonable doubt whether any living thing is a human being. A human being, from the moment of fertilization, is genetically complete. To quote professor Jerome Lejeune: "If a fertilized egg is not by itself a full human being, it could never become a man, because something would have to be added to it, and we know that does not happen."

When does human life begin? Biologically, this isn't a tough question. Regardless of whether one ultimately supports legalized abortion, it is a scientific fact that human life begins when a sperm fertilizes an egg. Once joined, the combination forms a new individual human possessing its own unique genetic code. The chromosomal composition of the newly formed individual remains unchanged whether it is permitted to reach maturity in the form of an infant at nine months or is terminated prematurely at six weeks. And, of course, if not aborted, the zygote inevitably grows into a human baby—not a frog, a cow, or a chicken.

What's the difference between a seven-day-old fetus and an eight-and-a-half-month-old fetus? If an eight-and-a-half-month-old fetus is a human entitled to legal protection, then why isn't a seven-day-old fetus entitled to the same protection? They both have the same unique genetic composition.

Humanity is not something one acquires, like a skill; you're either human or you're not. People may undergo socialization, societies may undergo civilization, but a human being cannot undergo humanization.

LIBERAL LUNACY:

"The decision to have an abortion is a personal choice of the woman and the government should stay out of it."

This begs the ultimate question of whether the fetus is a human life. If a fetus is human, nobody has a right to kill it. This argument is like saying that you should have the personal choice to commit murder or rape and the government shouldn't interfere.

LIBERAL LUNACY:
"We should strive to make abortion 'safe, legal, and rare'!"

That's Bill Clinton's phrase: "safe, legal, and rare."[1] He succeeded in keeping abortions "legal" and "safe" (for the mother, that is, not for her unborn child) but he didn't do anything to make abortion "rare." Today, one million abortions occur each year in the U.S. But why does it matter to Clinton (or any other liberal) that abortions are "rare," if aborting a fetus has the same moral significance as cutting your toenails?

LIBERAL LUNACY:
"Anti-abortion crusaders should not try 'to impose their religious views on others.'"

So the liberals want to eliminate religion from politics. Well, let's kiss goodbye those laws against murder and theft; after all, we derived them from the Ten Commandments. I guess we'll have to bring back slavery too: The movement to outlaw it was driven largely by Northeastern abolitionists inspired by Judeo-Christian ethics. Anyway, there is no religious creed that states: "The life of a human being

> A "partial-birth abortion" is defined in the Partial Birth Abortion Ban Act of 2003 as the killing of a fetus at least twenty weeks old and whose entire head is outside of the mother's body.

starts at fertilization, when the father's sperm unites with the mother's egg."[4] This is a sentence found not in the Bible but in a medical school textbook. The reason is simple. This is not a matter of faith, but of scientific fact. To call the results of this research "religious belief" is to call biology a religion.

The hard facts on abortion

- Until the twentieth century, state laws outlawing abortion were the norm in the United States.

- In 1965, the U.S. Supreme Court decided *Griswold v. Connecticut*, which recognized constitutional rights to privacy and to use contraception.

- By 1970, fourteen states had laws permitting abortion in certain circumstances.

- In 1973, the U.S. Supreme Court decided *Roe v. Wade*, which found that the constitutional "right to privacy" protected a woman's decision to have an abortion. *Roe v. Wade* legalized abortion on demand during the first three months of pregnancy.

- Child abuse has increased since *Roe v. Wade*, despite the fact that over twenty million abortions have taken place—which eliminated presumably potential "unwanted," supposedly abuse-prone children.[2] Since 1980, the incidence of child abuse has doubled.[3]

- In 2003, President Bush signed the Partial Birth Abortion Ban Act, which had passed both the Senate and the House. A day later, three federal judges issued restraining orders to prevent the enforcement of the new law.

LIBERAL LUNACY:
"Every child should be a planned and wanted child. No child should be born unwanted."

"Wantedness" is a subjective measure of another's feelings. If a child can't be allowed to live unless or until he is wanted, this makes human life not valuable in itself. No one's life has value unless others deem it valuable. Following this line of liberal logic, the homeless probably aren't "wanted," either. Should we do away with them?

Every baby should be wanted—simply because every baby is in fact a human being. If he isn't wanted, the problem lies with his parents or society at large, not with the innocent baby. Why should babies have to die because of the selfishness of others? Contrary to the old pro-abortion promise that legal abortion would lower the number of "unwanted" children and thus reduce child abuse, if anything, the opposite has occurred. Despite the fact that over twenty million presumably unwanted children have been killed by abortion since *Roe* v. *Wade*, the incidence of child abuse has doubled.[5] Since 1980, legalized abortion has resulted in the devaluing of human life such that the birth of a former fetus is viewed by many as the result of just another lifestyle choice, rather than a sacred event.

LIBERAL LUNACY:
"We're not pro-abortion, we're pro-choice."

This is a clever rhetorical dodge and nothing more. In practice, if you're not expressly against abortion, you are at least implicitly in favor of it. What if a group appeared in America tomorrow advocating the legalization of slavery, and explaining: "We're not in favor of slavery. We just want

the right to choose whether to own one." Everyone would recognize that this group was really pro-slavery. Any attempt to portray the "pro-choice" stance as abortion-neutral is just as ridiculous. Pro-choice groups can hardly be described as observers standing on the abortion sidelines.

Also, saying that one is in favor of the "choice" to abort assumes that abortion is a valid moral choice, just as being pro-choice on slavery necessarily involves assuming that slavery is not immoral.

VRWC TALKING POINTS

Every baby should be wanted—if he or she isn't, the problem lies with the parents or with society, not with the innocent new life. Why should children die for the selfishness of others?

★ From the moment of fertilization the fetus or child is imbued with its own unique genetic DNA code that will remain unaltered for the rest of its life—whether terminated by an abortion just three weeks later or by a natural death eighty years later.

★ Do you ask a pregnant mother, "How is your fetus?" or do you ask, "How is your baby?"

★ Let's assume your elderly grandfather is in a coma and you are asked whether to remove life support. Would the morality of your decision be altered if you knew that after nine months (the term of a normal pregnancy), he would regain consciousness and resume a normal life?[6]

YOU'VE GONE A LONG WAY OFF THE DEEP END, BABY: WHY EVERY WOMAN SHOULD REJECT RADICAL FEMINISM

Liberals uphold feminism as another great moral crusade. But if that were true, why do radical feminists care more about getting a handful of rich women into the Augusta National Golf Club than about destroying Saddam's government, which practiced an official policy of raping women as punishment?

★ ★ ★ ★ ★

Here's what the liberals say. . .

LIBERAL LUNACY:
"Women need government to protect them from discrimination in the workplace."

Yes, some men (primarily men who came of age before women entered the universities and workplace in great numbers) may be male chauvinist pigs who think that women are an inferior species. Many of these men are now retiring from the workplace. Soon they will be gone, leaving in their place younger men who attended schools and training programs alongside women. Remember, women have only been in the workforce in significant numbers (aside from during World War II) for about thirty years. After all, the women's liberation movement started in the 1960s.

Anyway, government intervention is not the answer to lingering gender discrimination in the workplace. Just as in the case of racial preferences, the government riding to the rescue of women sends the false message that women cannot succeed on their own merits. Moreover (and perhaps more damaging), government intervention discounts the achievements and struggles of those women who have

---

Feminist history

- In 1920, the Constitution was amended to give women the right to vote in federal elections—though women had been given the right to vote in many states much earlier.

- During World War II, women went to work in the factories to keep America's war machine running as the men fought the war. When the men returned, the vast majority of women left the workforce to get married and have children.

- In the 1960s, technological advances, modern appliances, and the birth control pill led young women to go to college in greater numbers and eventually to seek out roles in the workplace.

- In 1963, Betty Friedan's *The Feminine Mystique* started the "women's liberation movement." The overarching idea of the movement was that "[a]ll this social, occupational, educational, and political independence should yield economic independence and equality."[1]

made it without a "helping hand." This is the wrong message to send to society in general—and to women in particular. Women should be encouraged to do well and should be given an equal playing field, insofar as this means that the law should treat men and women equally. Laws classifying women as "minorities," providing them with special subsidies or assistance, only perpetuate the traditional patriarchal view that women (unlike men) need a helping hand.

LIBERAL LUNACY:
"Women make less money than men for the same work."

This argument comes only from liberals who have spent so much time taking womyn's studies courses that they've forgotten (or never learned) basic economics. Businesses exist to make profits. If they fail to earn profits, they die. The discipline imposed by the free market upon businesses creates an incentive to hire the best and brightest people in order to maximize profits and minimize the risk of going bankrupt. Since business owners want to avoid bankruptcy, they always try to hire the best workers they can afford in order to maximize their profits. They don't care about the sex or race of their workers—as long as those workers help the owners make money. If they fire competent blacks or women but keep incompetent white guys, their business will soon feel the pinch in profits. And if their competition is smart, they'll hire the competent black person or woman. Soon, the racist, sexist company will be history.

This is why the argument advanced by liberals that women get paid only 75 cents for every dollar a man makes is silly. If a company could cut its labor costs by 25

> " The ideology of feminism teaches that women have been mistreated since time began and that even in America women are discriminated against by an oppressive male-dominated society. As a political movement, feminism teaches that a just society must mandate identical treatment for men and women in every phase of our lives, no matter how reasonable it is to treat them differently, and that gender must never be used as the criterion for any decision. As an economic movement, feminism teaches that true fulfillment and liberation for women are in a paying job rather than in the confining, repetitious drudgery of the home, and that child care must not be allowed to interfere with a women's career. Feminism's psychological outlook on life is basically negative; it teaches women that the odds are stacked so severally against them that they probably cannot succeed in whatever they attempt.[2] "
>
> —Phyllis Schlafly

percent by hiring only women, every man in America would be out of work tomorrow. Heck, I'd even fire myself and get a woman to replace me!

The serious statistical work in this area corroborates this common sense point. Childless women working for the same consecutive periods of time as men earn the about the same or even more than men. The "wage gap" is simply a myth. According to Pacific Research Institute fellows Katherine Post and Michael Lynch, "The wage gap between women aged twenty-four to thirty-three who have never had children is virtually nonexistent compared to men of the same age. And a 1993 U.S.

Census Study shows that women who work at full-time jobs and have never married earn $1,005 for every $1,000 of their male counterparts." Post and Lynch say that as far back as the 1970s, never-married women in their thirties who worked continuously outearned never-married men: "There is vast evidence that women who chose to remain single, invest in education, and work long hours have in the past and continue to fare about as well as men in the labor market."

However, women who take substantial periods of time off from their career do generally make less money than men who have worked continuously without interruption. This should surprise nobody. If a man and a woman graduate from college together, but five years later, the woman takes three years off from work while the man keeps working, the man will have three additional years of work experience. That's likely to make him three years more valuable to his employer—thus explaining the discrepancy in pay.

LIBERAL LUNACY:
"Women can never get ahead of men because women are the only ones who can bear children, which inevitably hurts their careers."

In addressing this point, it's important to keep in mind that, at least for most people, deciding on a career path is not just about money. There are tradeoffs. Want to rise to the level of CEO in a Fortune 100 company? All right—but this will require many long days, late nights, weekend work, lots of travel, and many years of long, laborious, stressful toil. That price is more than most people (men or women) want to pay.

That people choose not to stay on such a career path is no one's business but their own. That some women or men decide to step off the career path leading to the highest-paying and most prestigious jobs in America because they don't want to run in the corporate rat race speaks highly of American society. In America, we each have the choice to work as hard (or as little) as we like and to place family above work, or vice versa. If women (or men) decide to spend more time with their family and less time at work, then great for them!

LIBERAL LUNACY:
"Without feminism, women would be stuck being housewives."

Feminists denigrate women who stay home. They place a much higher value upon individual women succeeding in the workplace and in the political arena. Conservatives, in contrast, believe that all men and women should be free to choose their own life paths, and that the decision to stay home and raise a family is as admirable as working as a high-powered professional.

Indeed, the raising of children may be the single most important job a parent will ever have. Says the eloquent Judge Robert Bork: "It should be a source of great pride to bear the next generation and to train that generation's minds and morals. That is certainly a greater accomplishment than churning out tracts raging at men and families. It is fine that women are taking up careers, but the price from that need not be the demoralization of women who do not choose that path."[3]

Anyway, women owe the feminist movement nothing. It was advancing technology, not feminism, which paved the way for women to enter the workplace in large numbers. Technological advances like the vacuum cleaner, the dishwasher, the birth control pill, and the microwave oven had more to do with women working outside the home than the rantings of Betty Friedan or the National Organization of Women.[4] The free market—not any liberal academic musings—is responsible for this technological revolution and the betterment of women (and men) everywhere.

VRWC TALKING POINTS

Women in the U.S. today enjoy more freedoms, rights, professional success, and opportunities than at any other moment in history or place in the world. Consider:

★ Women are not "minorities" in America. Women constitute 52 percent of the voting populating and outnumber men in all but two states.

★ Women hold more than half of the wealth in the U.S., and make up over half the college students in the country and over half the applicants to medical and law schools.

★ Contrary to radical feminist attitudes, women who chose to place family over their careers should be admired as much as any high-powered professional.

PLUCKING CHICKEN LITTLE: A COMMON-SENSE APPROACH TO THE ENVIRONMENT

Liberals have warned us about overpopulation only to see the world's population growth plummeting—in Europe it's below replacement level. Liberals warned us about mass global starvation—while in fact the world now sits on food surpluses. Liberals warned us about a coming Ice Age—but now they say the real danger is global warming. Would you trust someone who's repeatedly made such wrong doomsday predictions?

★ ★ ★ ★ ★

Here's what the liberals say. . .

LIBERAL LUNACY:
"Conservatives don't care about the environment."

Conservatives want to protect the environment as much as our Birkenstock-wearing liberal friends. But conservatives don't base their environmental policies on emotions, hysteria, or junk science. Dinesh D'Souza said it best: Conservatives "like trees, rivers, and baby seals as much as the next guy," but caring for the environment "does not require Americans to walk lockstep with the radical environmentalist agenda."[1]

Environmentalists, perhaps weaned on too many *Star Trek* episodes, are frequently incapable of distinguishing between science fiction and science fact. Indeed, the scare tactics and scapegoating so often employed by liberal environmentalists tend to undermine support for environmental causes and, even worse, may serve to discredit actual threats to health and safety.

After all, liberals have been playing Chicken Little for decades. They predicted that the earth was running out of food and water. They were wrong. They predicted that pollution levels would not fall. They were wrong. They claimed that the world's population was growing so fast that it would outstrip the world's capacity to feed them. Wrong again. They claimed that reserves of oil and fossil fuels would cease to exist. Nope. They even claimed that the Earth was about to plunge into an ice age—that one was before the opposite hysterical claim, global warming, caught on. Al Gore even proposed abolishing the internal combustion engine.

How can anybody take these people seriously?

LIBERAL LUNACY:
"Industrial growth harms the environment."

Wrong. You know what's really bad for the environment? An environmental policy designed to punish business and the economy. In reality, the "corporate polluters" and oil companies are leading the way in environmental cleanup.

Environmentalists may be well intentioned, but their policies hurt people by destroying jobs and damaging the economy. Look around the world: Countries that are economic basket cases are also environmental nightmares. Just compare the "free market" U.S. with the once centrally planned countries of the former Soviet Union. In countries where the economies are relatively free from government interference, the natural environment is cleaner than in countries with state-controlled economies. Also, wealthier countries can afford to worry about environmental sustainability, and can afford the necessary technology; poor countries can't.

Save the purple bankclimber mussel!

- The Endangered Species Act is a prime example of regulation run amok. Enacted to preserve the habitats of endangered species, most Americans thought its purpose was to save baby seals, manatees, and other furry, fuzzy creatures from Walt Disney movies. But get this: Most of the species listed as endangered and thus entitled to protection under the Endangered Species Act are invertebrates and insects.

- Of the 388 animals listed as endangered here in the U.S., only sixty-five are mammals. The remaining 323 animals include sixty-two types of clams, twenty-one types of snail, thirty-five types of insect, and seventy-one types of fish.

- When children send in dollar bills as part of school projects to protect endangered species, we can sleep soundly knowing that they are helping to save the purple bankclimber mussel, which has been listed as a federally protected endangered species since 1998.

Private companies have an incentive to keep the environment clean. It's called "profits." Before a company can consume resources in order to produce its product, the company has to buy the resources. The fewer resources it has to buy to make its product, the lower its costs are, and the higher its profits. Soft drink cans illustrate this. "In the 1960s, when most soft-drink cans were made of steel, making one thousand cans required 164 pounds of metal. By 1990, the same number of cans could be made from only thirty-five pounds of aluminum."[2] In an attempt to make more money, the companies sought to reduce their production costs by switching from steel to aluminum, and then sought to use less aluminum. The result? The use of fewer natural resources—without the coercive hand of government.

> ### CONVERSATION STOPPER
>
> Look around the world: Countries that are economic basket cases are also environmental nightmares. In countries where the economies are relatively free from government interference, the natural environment is cleaner than in countries with state-controlled economies.

LIBERAL LUNACY:

"America produces 25 percent of the world's carbon dioxide, causing global warming. We should enact laws to reduce that amount."

They won't tell you this in the *New York Times*, but we don't even know if carbon dioxide actually affects the Earth's temperature. So the amount of carbon dioxide America puts out may well be completely insignificant. If radical environmentalists had taken time out from being environmentally active to read up on some "hard" science, they would know this.

And anyway, the world needs carbon dioxide–based products. News flash to the Left: Carbon dioxide is not a poison or pollutant. Trees and plants need carbon dioxide to survive—so they must love America! And what are we doing that makes all this carbon dioxide? Producing things the world wants and needs: food products, medicine, technology, and more.

As for global warming, it still isn't proven. A fundamental problem with the global warming debate is that there is no easy way to determine the temperature of the Earth. If you compare temperatures in cities today with data from twenty-five or fifty years ago, how can you be sure that that's enough to tell you anything reliable? What was the temperature in your city one hundred years ago? During the Dark Ages? At the time of Christ? During the days of Socrates, or Dino the Dinosaur?

Okay, it's true that over the last one hundred years, the average world temperature has probably gone up about 1 degree Fahrenheit.[3] However, we don't know if the rise is due to natural variation or anything relating to people.[4] Liberals love to think that the increase of carbon dioxide, which is created by the burning of fossil fuels such as coal and oil, is causing the atmosphere to warm up due to the "greenhouse effect." But we just don't know. We do know that "if [carbon dioxide] and other greenhouse gases caused the Earth to warm, temperatures should have risen roughly in tandem with the increase in greenhouse gases."[5] However, over the last century, "the pattern of warming does not follow the rise of [carbon dioxide]."[6]

That's right, though carbon dioxide has been increasing steadily, average global temperatures have not. Seems to raise a question about causation, huh?

Earth has been around for a very long time, and humans have been here for only a fraction of it. Now, environmentalists would have us believe that in the span of about one hundred years there is sufficient evidence to prove that humans are causing this 3.5 billion-year-old planet to warm up to cataclysmic temperatures. Sorry, but I just don't buy it.

What about the "hole in the ozone layer," you ask? There again: not enough data. Scientists have been measuring the ozone on Earth only since 1956. What we're experiencing now could be a completely natural phenomenon.

Nor do we even know if global warming would be bad. Thomas Gale Moore, a senior fellow at the Hoover Institution and author of *Climate of Fear: Why We Shouldn't Worry about Global Warming*, explains that a warmer Earth might be welcome. Moore explains that a warmer planet could give a "rising world population longer growing seasons, greater rainfall, and an enriched atmosphere" helpful in staving off famines. Moore explains also that while "most economic activities would be unaffected by climate change" (since most such activities occur indoors in heated or air-conditioned climates), some outdoor-oriented services could be benefited. "Transportation would benefit generally from a warmer climate, since road transport would suffer less from slippery or impassable highways. Airline passengers, who often endure weather-related delays in the winter, would gain from more reliable and on-time service."[7]

Even the Democrats are hesitant to adopt extremist environmental agenda. The proposed Kyoto Treaty, which would have required signatory nations to significantly cut "greenhouses gases" resulting from the burning of fossil fuels, was rejected by the U.S. Senate by a 95–0 vote. Why? Because ratifying the treaty would have required a large reduction in the use of the fossil fuels that we use to run our economy. Until there is an alternative fuel source that is better than good old-fashioned coal and oil, restricting our economy's ability to burn these fuels will only hurt economic growth.

> 66 Although there are now twice as many of us as there were in 1961, each of us has more to eat, in both developed and developing countries. Fewer people are starving. Food is far cheaper these days and food-wise the world is quite simply a better place for far more people. 99
>
> —Bjørn Lomborg, author of *The Skeptical Environmentalist*

Better check with Al Gore—he just gave a speech on global warming in New York City on what turned out to be one of the coldest days in the city's history.

LIBERAL LUNACY:
"We are running out of energy, food, and natural resources."

Here we go again. Radical environmental activists are long on emotional rhetoric and short on scientific fact. "Contrary to the predictions of many environmentalist ideologues," says analyst Norman Borlaug, "world food supplies have more than tripled in the past thirty years, staying well ahead of world population growth. Global food supplies, if equitably distributed, could provide an adequate diet for 700 million more people than there are living in the world today."[8]

Fewer and fewer people are starving, and there will be more and more food per person in the future. Poverty has been reduced in virtually every country.[9] Fewer people worldwide are starving: In 1970, 35 percent of those living in developing countries were starving; in 1996, it was down to 18 percent. The United Nations expects this to fall to 12 percent by 2010.[10]

Just check your local supermarket. Walk the aisles. You'll see rows and rows of groceries of all types. Prices are generally low. Western countries, especially the United States, are far more worried about overeating than starving. As Bjørn Lomborg explains in *The Skeptical Environmentalist*, "Although there are now twice as many of us as there were in 1961, each of us has more to eat, in both developed and developing countries. Fewer people are starving. Food is far cheaper these days and food-wise the world is quite simply a better place for far more people."[11]

To the extent that starvation still exists in Africa and elsewhere, the fault lies with shortsighted and self-serving (and generally hard-Left) political leaders, rather than with the world's supposed scarcity of natural resources. After all, people were malnourished in Saddam Hussein's Iraq not because of a lack of food (even during the embargo), but because of selfish opportunism, political jockeying, and outright theft by Saddam and his cronies.

Make no mistake: Our modern lifestyle is the radical environmentalists' ultimate target. Regardless of the issue—global warming, overpopulation, nuclear waste, the depletion of resources, the extinction of species—

environmentalists blame America and its wealth. They charge that the richer we get, the more irreplaceable resources we consume, and that as we consume them we pollute the Earth. The clear implication of all this is that the Earth would be better off without us.

VRWC TALKING POINTS

Liberal predictions of environmental disaster have been repeatedly, consistently, and always wrong. We are not running out of food, we did not have a new ice age, and chances are we won't suffer from global warming. Consider:

* People are living longer and better lives and the world is getting cleaner every day, thanks to the technological advancements, wealth accumulation, and economic growth inherent in free market economies.

* The natural environment is better off under free market capitalist economies than under heavily regulated controlled ones. Think Chernobyl.

DON'T LET HILLARY CHOOSE YOUR OB/GYN: THE CASE AGAINST GOVERNMENT-CONTROLLED HEALTH CARE

In Canada, home of socialized health care, doctors boast that "most" urgent care patients are treated within two weeks.[1] Do you want to have a heart attack in a country that boasts that "most" urgent patients are treated within two weeks?

★ ★ ★ ★ ★

Here's what the liberals say. . .

LIBERAL LUNACY:
"Americans spend too much money on health care."

How do liberals know how much money each of us should spend on health care? Should we be spending 5 percent of our income? 10 percent? 40 percent? Should the percentage change as we get older? You can't know whether someone is really spending a "disproportionate" amount on something unless you know exactly what is the "correct" or "proportionate" amount. But nobody knows that. If anything, Americans spend too much money on fatty foods, alcohol, cigarettes, and all sorts of other fun things that liberal puritans want us to shun.

In reality, there is no health care crisis in America. Americans have access to the greatest health care system in the world—as shown by the fact that Americans (despite the fast-food joints and beer) live about as long as anyone else on the planet. We have been blessed with this great health care system not because God, the United Nations, or the U.S. Congress willed it. We have a great health care system because it allows those working within the system (doctors, nurses, medical and scientific researchers, and pharmaceutical companies) to make profits. In nations that have implemented socialist health care systems (i.e., Canada and the United Kingdom), the quality of health care—and access to it—is far inferior to that in the United States.

Still, the debate about health care isn't going away as long as Hillary continues to mull over a White House run. So it's important to remember that he who pays the bills is the boss. Whoever is in charge of paying for health care in America will ultimately be responsible for the type and quality of care Americans receive. If you pay for your own health care, either directly or through your insurance plan, then the doctors and medical professionals who serve you are, in effect, your employees. But if the government pays for your health care, then you're not the boss anymore. Whether doctors treat you well or poorly, they'll get the same salary. If the government pays for all the health care in America, then count on your local doctor and hospital being as responsive to your needs as your local Department of Motor Vehicles.

Anyway, in many important ways America already has a socialized health care system. Insured taxpayers already have to pay both for their own health insurance and for the insurance of those who are poor (Medicaid), elderly (Medicare) or uninsured altogether (the cost of their emergency room visits gets built into the insured's taxes or insurance premiums). Allowing Americans to acquire health care outside of any socialized system will continue to be important in the same way that private schools are important: It's an issue of quality as much as it is one of freedom.

LIBERAL LUNACY:
"Too many Americans are uninsured."

Here it comes again: So what? Let me play the heartless conservative of liberal myth for a minute and ask: Who cares if we have uninsured people? There's not a word in the U.S. Constitution that grants you the right to health insurance. If you want health insurance, buy it. If you don't, why must your neighbors buy it for you?

Oh, but people will die, you say? Heartless doctors will refuse to treat impoverished patients, leaving them to die on hospital doorsteps? Nope. Doesn't happen. Although not all Americans have health insurance, they do have universal access to health care—which is obviously far more important than having insurance. Under federal law, hospital emergency rooms are required to treat anyone, including the uninsured.[2] Thus Americans already have universal health care.

LIBERAL LUNACY:
"Why can't we have universal
health care like Canada or Great Britain?

This question ignores the fact that, as I just explained, we already have universal health care. What liberals are really asking is why can't we have socialist, government-controlled health care. Well, we can. But we don't want it.

In Canada, home of socialized health care, doctors brag about how urgent cases get treatment in a timely manner—that is, they're treated "within two weeks."[3] Hey, Canucks, that's terrific! But I think that, all things considered, I don't want to get sick or hurt in a nation with such a system. Say you hurt your knee playing in a football game, and your doctor recommends you get an MRI. If you happen to live in Canada, you'll find that the wait for an MRI is several months. But if you happen to live in the United States, you'll be able to get an MRI within a week. In which country would you prefer to hurt your knee?

Royalty from Middle Eastern countries like Saudi Arabia have long come to the U.S. for medical treatment. Why not Canada or Britain? Because they know that America has the world's finest health care system. (This is an interesting phenomenon. By taking advantage of U.S. health care, aren't these Arab princes delaying their big party in Paradise with all those virgins?)

LIBERAL LUNACY:
"Health care is not like other goods or services. People will consume only what they need and not what they want."

Au contraire, if you'll pardon my French. Harvard University professor Joseph Newhouse conducted a study over the medical spending habits of almost 8,000 people in the United States. He wanted to find out whether asking people to pay in part for their own health care caused a reduction in their demand for health care, and whether their decisions, if any, to forego health care resulted in harm to their health. The results were startling to liberals—but not to anyone who understands the basic rules of supply and demand. The study found that those who had to pay for their health care consumed 50 percent fewer medical services than those who received the same services for free. Also, those who received "free" health care had hospital admission rates 30–50 percent higher than those who actually had to pay something for their health care.

> ### CONVERSATION STOPPER
>
> If the government pays for all the health care in America, then expect your local doctor and hospital to be as responsive to your needs as your local Department of Motor Vehicles.

But did those who went without health care suffer for it? Nope. The study concluded that "the average person's health changed very little, despite the rather large change in use caused by the insurance plans."[4]

LIBERAL LUNACY:

"It's not fair for some people to get fantastic health care while other get lesser care."

This is another example of the famous liberal last resort: the appeal to envy. Why should a successful business person get to drive a 2004 SUV while a schoolteacher has to drive a VW bug? Why shouldn't someone get the best care possible if he wants it and can afford it? This is just another manifestation of liberals' hatred of the rich. But there has never been and never will be a society in which everyone has the same amount of everything. Human nature just isn't designed that way.

VRWC TALKING POINTS

Americans have available to them the best doctors, hospitals, drugs, and health care in the world. Why mess with the best?

★ In nations with socialist health care systems (e.g. Canada and Britain), the quality of health care—and access to it—is far inferior to that in America. Why? When the government takes over paying for health care, health care providers work for the government and not for you, the consumer. At that point, expect to be treated the same way you get treated when you visit your local Department of Motor Vehicles.

★ Universal health care already exists; federal law mandates emergency care.

★ American pharmaceutical companies develop lifesaving drugs because they are motivated by profits—developing the drugs that people really need.

STOPP SUPORTING PUBLIK SKOOLS: DEFENDING SCHOOL CHOICE

Who cares more about your children—you or the government? Who is responsible for your children—you or the government? Whose values should be imparted to your children—yours or the government's? And who should decide where your kids go to school—you or the government?

* * * * *

Here's what the liberals say. . .

LIBERAL LUNACY:
"We must spend more taxpayer money on public schools in order to raise teacher salaries and reduce class size."

When businesses fail to provide a desirable service to customers, they go out of business. But when a government program fails, the government asks for more and more money. That's what's happening with public schools today: the country's worst school districts generally have the highest per-student spending. The District of Columbia spends about $10,000 every year per student. That's three times more than it spent in 1963. But what does all this money buy? Not much: in virtually every indicator of student performance (i.e. math, science, and reading proficiency), Washington, D.C., public school students rank at the bottom, or near it.[1]

If anyone can be forgiven for giving up on public schools, it would be parents in Washington. These parents have a responsibility to make sure their kids are properly educated. How can the government help? By giving them back the tax money they spend on failed public schools.

LIBERAL LUNACY:
"It takes a village to raise a child. Education is a community responsibility, best discharged by educational experts in public schools."

No, Hillary, it really doesn't take a village to raise a child, except maybe in the socialist paradise of your dreams. In fact, it just takes parents. Liberals think that only state-supported teachers know how to educate your child properly. (Last I checked, the prestigious Ivy League colleges were all private.) School vouchers would prevent these public school teachers from carrying out their liberal socialist experiment on our children: teaching them to hate America, distrust their parents, and believe that big government is the solution to all of society's ailments.

Parents—not government educrats—should decide how to raise their kids, and where and how to educate them. Parents should be able to decide how money is spent on their children's education. After all, it's their money. If parents want to send their child to a private school, they should not also have to subsidize the schooling of other families' children. "In a nation supposedly committed to free enterprise,

Where's the "choice" in education?

- Liberals are always talking about "choice" when it comes to abortion; why not in education? The answer is simple: teacher unions don't want the competition.

- The public school monopoly has been largely taken over by teachers' unions—the National Education Association (NEA) and the American Federation of Teachers (AFT)—who are more interested in the welfare of their members and not the welfare of the children.[2]

- America's largest teachers union has made up the largest single group of delegates at every Democratic National Convention since 1980. Teacher union-affiliated delegates nowadays out-number California's entire delegation.[3]

- In 1996, 363 DNC delegates were NEA members. Another 117 delegates were affiliated with the AFT. This means more than 10 percent of the delegates who nominated President Clinton for a second term were unionized teachers.

- Today, the NEA has about 2.4 million members and the American Federation of Teachers has about one million members. The NEA budget for its national office in 1998–99 was approximately $221 million. Here are the millionaires who want to deny many children a quality education.[4]

consumer choice, and equal educational opportunities," constitutional attorney Clint Bolick declares, "school choice should be routine. That it is not demonstrates the clout and determination of those dedicated to preserving the government's monopoly over public education."[5]

LIBERAL LUNACY:
"Vouchers are crazy, untested experiments."

This argument is a joke. School choice isn't new any more than consumer choice in a free market economy is new. Voluntary non-compulsory schools were in the U.S. long before public schools became the norm. Today, millions of Americans who can afford to do so send their children to private and parochial schools. In those schools, they usually receive an education superior to the one they'd get in a public school. Today, one out of every ten parents in the U.S. sends their children to private school.[6] Says attorney Clint Bolick: "[P]rivate schools, often using public funds, have played a key role in American education. Even today, America's post-secondary system of education—the world's envy—is characterized by widespread school choice. Students can use the G.I. Bill, Pell Grants, and other forms of government aid to attend either public or private schools, including religious institutions. Parents can use childcare vouchers in private and religious settings. Indeed, under federal law, tens of thousands of disabled children receive schooling in private schools at public expense. It is only mainstream K-12 schools in which the government commands a monopoly over public funds."[7]

Moreover, voucher programs are "experimental" and "untested" because professional educators and bureaucrats are fighting relentlessly against any efforts to start school choice programs. Why? Government educrats realize that their product can't compete in the free market. Once school vouchers become available, the educrats will hear the thunder of young feet racing out the doors of their schools to schools where it's still possible to get an education.

In fact, an educational marketplace is ready and waiting. Students today have many educational options, if the government school monopoly would just step aside. "The pre-collegiate education system in the United States is a mosaic of public, religious, independent, and other private schools, all working together to provide the best possible education for American children. A system that relies on the richness of pluralism and diversity must make its resources accessible to all children. A basic belief of private education is that families should have options in the pursuit of their children's education. Such choices always have existed for families that have the means to pay private school tuition costs, and should be available to all."[8]

> ### CONVERSATION STOPPER
>
> A poll conducted in 2000 by the Washington-based Center for Education Reform found that 70 percent of African-American parents earning less than $15,000 a year support school choice.[10]

Also, vouchers work. "For more than a century, Vermont has operated a viable and popular voucher system in ninety towns across the state. During the 1998–99 school year, the state paid tuition for 6,505 students in kindergarten through twelfth grade to attend public and private schools. Families chose from a large pool of public schools and more than eighty-three independent schools, including such well-known academies as Phillips Exeter and Holderness. . . . Vermont's voucher program has been running since 1869, nearly as long as the monopolistic public education model."[9]

LIBERAL LUNACY:
"We must have public schools to give
minority children a chance to get an education."

Unfortunately for liberals, school choice is supported by one of their core constituencies: inner-city minorities. Many black and other minority parents support school choice programs because they and their children have suffered the most in failing public schools. Recently, U.S. Supreme Court Justice Clarence Thomas wrote, "[t]oday many of our inner-city public schools deny emancipation to urban minority students," who "have been forced into a system that continually fails them."

Minority and low-income parents express overwhelming support for parental choice, and are most interested in placing their children in private schools. Says Terry Moe of the Hoover Institution: "[T]he appeal of private schools is especially strong among parents who are low in income, minority, and live in low-performing districts: precisely the parents who are the most disadvantaged under the current system."[11]

The strongest support for vouchers, notes Moe, comes from people who are socially less advantaged, members of minority groups, and residents of low-performing school districts. Survey after survey confirms this. A poll conducted in 2000 by the Washington-based Center for Education Reform found that 70 percent of African-American parents earning less than $15,000 a year support school choice.[12]

The reasons for this are obvious. A black high school dropout earns just over $13,500, but with a high school degree, the average income of blacks rises to almost $21,000. Blacks with a bachelor's degree have an average annual income of about $37,500, and $75,500 with a professional degree.[13] Staying in school—and getting out of the chaotic war zones that are all too many public schools today—has obvious benefits.

VRWC TALKING POINTS

It takes parents (not a village) to raise a child—parents, not educrats, should decide how and where to educate their children. A child's education is far too important to be left to failing government schools. Parents get to decide what their children eat, wear, and play, so why shouldn't all parents, including poor ones, be given the opportunity to decide where to educate their children?

* Liberals such as Bill and Hillary Clinton, Al Gore, Ted Kennedy, and Jesse Jackson refused to send *their own children* to public schools. What does this say about the quality of public schools?

* We already spend massive amounts of money on public schools. The District of Columbia spends about $10,000 every year per student, yet its public school students rank among the bottom of the nation.

* Good old-fashioned free market competition gives consumers more choices in products at lower prices. The education marketplace is no different, as we see with colleges and universities. Give parents vouchers to select their children's school and we'll see better schools at lower costs.

* Seventy percent of African-American parents earning less than $15,000 a year support school choice.

GUNS DON'T KILL PEOPLE: LIBERAL GUN CONTROL LAWS KILL PEOPLE

If guns don't deter crimes, then why do armed Secret Service agents surround the president?

★ ★ ★ ★ ★

Here's what the liberals say...

LIBERAL LUNACY:
"The Second Amendment confers no individual right to own guns but merely allows states to keep a militia, which today is taken care of by the National Guard."

First, how about reading the thing? The Second Amendment says that "the people" shall have the right to keep and bear arms. In interpreting "the people" as it is used in the Second, Fourth, Ninth, and Tenth Amendments, the Supreme Court has made it clear again and again that it refers to individuals.[1]

Let's also not forget that the Second Amendment falls in the middle of the Bill of Rights. So we're supposed to believe that stuck in the middle of all these constitutionally protected *individual* rights is one that grants powers to state governments? I don't think so. The Bill of Rights was written to set forth those rights of the individual so fundamental that they may not be infringed upon by government. If the Founders intended the Second Amendment to grant powers to state governments, they certainly put it in a funny place.

The Founders made the importance of an armed citizenry abundantly clear because they understood that the first step tyrannical governments take to oppress the citizenry is to disarm them. Why did Paul Revere ride through the Massachusetts countryside in 1775, warning that the British were coming? Was he worried that the British were marching to torch the countryside and rape the colonists? Hardly. The British were marching to seize the colonists' guns.

LIBERAL LUNACY:
"Guns are dangerous and should be banned."

Sure, guns are dangerous, but so are cars, planes, knives, hammers, and ropes. Criminals have used them all to commit heinous crimes. Criminals who use guns to murder, criminals who use automobiles as getaway cars, and terrorists who fly airplanes into buildings should all be punished. But it would be just as silly to call these "airplane crimes" or "car crimes" as it is to refer to "gun crimes." The focus should be the criminal, not the tool he used.

As many as 86 million people own over 200 million guns in the U.S. This includes about 60 million handguns. Of all these guns, only about 30,000 are involved in deaths each year—including deaths from murders, accidents, and suicides. That's .015 percent of all the guns in America.

As in all other areas, when talking about gun control, liberals don't consider the true costs of their policy proposals. They refuse to acknowledge the tremendous and well-documented benefits of civilian gun ownership. Many studies have demonstrated that Americans use guns to protect themselves, often stopping crimes without firing a shot.[2] In the largest study ever conducted on the effect of gun control laws, John R. Lott, Jr. studied crime data for every county in the U.S. He found that "when state concealed handgun laws went into effect in a county, murders fell by 8.5 percent, and rapes and aggravated assaults fell by 5 percent and 7 percent."

Also, gun control laws simply don't thwart criminals. Washington, D.C., banned handguns in 1976. By 1991, its homicide rate had tripled. In the same period, the homicide rate in the rest of the U.S. rose 12 percent—still a matter of grave concern, but a significantly smaller increase.

More recently, in October 2003, an independent task force of the U.S. Center for Disease Control and Prevention released a study finding no link whatsoever between gun control laws and lower crime rates. The study "conducted a systematic review of scientific evidence regarding the effectiveness of firearms laws in preventing violence, including violent crimes, suicide, and unintentional injury"

> ## CONVERSATION STOPPER
>
> Criminals use guns to murder, cars to get away, knives, hammers, and ropes to break in, and even airplanes to bring down buildings. The focus should be the criminal, not the tool he used.

and *"found insufficient evidence to determine the effectiveness of any of the firearms laws or combinations of laws reviewed on violent outcomes."*[3]

Passing yet another gun control law to add to the already existing 20,000 gun laws already on the books won't do any good. Enacting a law that expressly prohibits hijacking an airplane and flying it into a building wouldn't have stopped the 9/11 attacks, which, obviously, violated many existing laws. Likewise, a criminal who intends to commit murder with a firearm has already decided to break the law. The fact that he may also violate a gun law will not deter him from committing murder.

LIBERAL LUNACY:
"Guns kill children. We've got to protect the children!"

It is always a tragedy when a child's life is needlessly cut short. Liberals embrace these opportunities to push for more gun control. But we have to be on guard that those senseless tragedies do not result in the erosion of our individual liberties. As a society, we must ask ourselves: In making laws that govern the behavior of adults, do we want to base the legal standard on a typical five-year-old? Should we accept the notion that every adult in the U.S. must give up the right to defend himself in order to prevent the potential misuse of guns (or any other product for that matter) by five-year-olds with irresponsible parents? Absolutely not. I like kids, but that's no way to run a society of free adults.

> **CONVERSATION STOPPER**
>
> More children under five drown in water buckets than children under ten die from accidental gunshots. Is it time for water bucket control laws?

Now, the obligation to protect children from dangers in the home falls to parents. A responsible parent will take steps to make his house safe for his kids. If a parent leaves a loaded gun or household chemicals around, it's his fault if his child is injured—not mine, not yours, not the law's. A society of over 220 million responsible, law-abiding adults should not be forced to surrender their freedoms because a few parents are careless.

Let's also look at the "kids and guns" statistics bandied about by the gun haters. Michael Barnes, then–president of Handgun Control, Inc., testified before the U.S. Senate that in the U.S. about eleven children a day die from gun violence. Is this true? Are eleven kids coming home from elementary school each day to watch Barney on TV, only to be killed by a gun? Of course not. Barnes is lumping teenage criminals in with the people he refers to as "children." Violent crime is largely a young man's game. Among "children" nineteen and under, in 2000 there were 3,012 gun-related deaths (including suicides and murders). If, however, you define "children" as four-teen-year-olds and younger, thereby excluding most gang members and teen drug dealers, there were only 433 total deaths. Though any death of an innocent child is tragic, this puts Barnes's hysterical claim in perspective.

Many objects kill far more children than guns.[4] In 1999, 1,260 children under ten died due to motor vehicles, 484 died in residential fires, ninety-three children under ten drowned in bathtubs, and another thirty-six children under five drowned in five-gallon plastic buckets. "More children under five drown in this one type of water bucket than children under ten die from any type of accidental gunshot."[5] Folks, it's time to put safety locks on the water buckets. Indeed, "[a]ccidental firearm deaths are at an all-time low, while gun ownership is at an all-time high."[6]

Of course, some liberals will argue that if banning guns saves just one child's life, then we should ban guns. But using the same logic, Americans use guns to defend themselves from at least 80,000 assaults, robberies, and household burglaries each year. At least one child's life is saved each year by gun ownership.

VRWC TALKING POINTS

In reality, gun control laws would leave millions of Americans defenseless against violent predators. That's not a society in which we'd want to live. Consider:

★ You have a right to life and thus a right to defend that life against criminal predators. Guns allow you to exercise this fundamental human right.

★ More guns mean less crime, as seen in study after study, including the largest study ever conducted. Researcher John R. Lott, Jr. demonstrated that "when state concealed handgun laws went into effect in a county, murders fell by 8.5 percent, and rapes and aggravated assaults fell by 5 percent and 7 percent."

★ In every state that has enacted a conceal carry law, making it easier for more law-abiding citizens to carry guns, crime rates plummet. After the right-to-carry law went into effect in Texas in 1996, the state murder rate fell by 60 percent within four years. After the right-to-carry law went into effect in Florida in 1987, Florida's homicide rate fell by 23 percent in five years (in contrast to the U.S. homicide rate, which rose 9 percent during that same period).

★ Of the 200 million guns in the U.S. today, only about .015 percent of all guns in America are involved in deaths each year.

IT'S SIMPLE: DO THE CRIME, SERVE THE TIME

Liberals believe that guns don't deter crime, harsh prison sentences don't deter crime, nothing, in fact, deters crime. We all just need more tolerance and understanding and government social programs. But ask a liberal this: Where would you rather see a career criminal living—behind bars or next door to your family?

★ ★ ★ ★ ★

Here's what the liberals say. . .

LIBERAL LUNACY:
"Criminals aren't responsible for their crimes. Society is."

We've bought into this way of thinking for decades now. During the 1960s and 1970s, we adopted a soft-on-crime approach advocated by liberal theorists. They insisted that people committed crimes not because they were criminals, but because they were poor, their mother dressed them funny, they didn't have puppies growing up, or because they were not being "raised by a village." These wrong-headed notions led to public policies, which denied the link between individual responsibility and criminal conduct.

The result of this kind of thinking? More criminals stayed on the streets for longer. In 1960, for every 1,000 violent crime arrests, 299 arrestees were eventually imprisoned. But by 1970, that number had fallen to 170.[1] Crime rates soared. From 1960 to 1970, violent crime rates rose 126 percent. In the next decade, they jumped another 64 percent.

But then the picture began to change. From 1980 to 1990, the violent crime rate went up again, but at a slower pace: 23 percent. Then violent crime rates actually began to fall—there was a 6.4 percent drop between 1990 and 1995.[2] Why did violent crime rates begin to drop? Because communities all across the U.S. started to roll back the destructive liberal policies of the sixties. Criminals began going to jail in greater numbers and for longer periods. In 1980, state and federal prisons held 329,821 inmates; by 1990, there were 773,919 prisoners, and by 1994, 1,053,738.[3] Liberals howled, but there was no mistaking the numbers. McGruff was starting to take a bite out of crime.

LIBERAL LUNACY:
"We should focus on eliminating the root cause of crime by expanding social programs and building more schools instead of more prisons."

Once again, liberals have the causal chain backwards. Poverty does not cause crime, but crime causes poverty. Liberals love to justify big government, higher taxes, and more social programs by saying, "People turn to crime because of social conditions: poverty, illegitimacy, and a lack of economic opportunities. If we just spend more taxpayer dollars for social programs, we can reduce crime rates." Sounds great. And saying it often enough might earn you a master's degree in Sociology or Womyn's Studies. But it sure won't do anything to save innocent lives from violent predators.

Let's look at the record: "Between 1962 and 1972, spending in America's twenty-eight largest cities increased 198 percent, while federal and state aid to cities rose 370 percent. Federal direct aid to cities rose from less than $1 billion a year in 1964 to $21 billion in 1980, finally leveling off under President Reagan."[4] With all that money pouring into the cities, the crime rate must have fallen sharply, right? It didn't!

> According to a 2002 study by the Department of Justice, approximately 68 percent of criminals released from federal prison are rearrested for a felony or serious misdemeanor within three years of their release. Almost 47 percent were convicted of a new crime.

In fact, crime skyrocketed. Cities like Washington, D.C., and New York City were first in line at the federal trough for welfare and social programs—and at the same time became showcases of violent crime and social disorder. Once again, if you subsidize socially undesirable behavior, you get more of it. The bottom line: Crime causes poverty, not the other way around. Businesses and productive law-abiding citizens leave neighborhoods when they become crime-ridden. They take jobs and economic opportunities with them. Potential employers and investors go elsewhere. Wouldn't you?

LIBERAL LUNACY:
"Getting tough on crime harms minorities."

Liberals say this because when arrests go up, arrests of blacks and other minorities go up. There is no doubt that crime rates are higher in minority communities than they are in the general population. Is that because of racism or profiling? Give me a break. Blacks and Hispanics can lower crime rates in the inner city by getting tough on crime. And they have very good reason to do so: according to the National Crime and Victimization Survey, Hispanics and blacks were both more likely than whites to become victims of violent crimes. Blacks were more than "three times more likely than whites to become victims of robbery, and twice as likely to become victims of aggravated assault, as whites."[5]

LIBERAL LUNACY:
"Those who commit crimes should get a chance to make something of their lives."

Sure they should. But this is no argument for letting violent or serial criminals out of prison quickly. After all, recidivism rates justify long prison sentences. Most violent criminals commit violent crimes soon after they are released from prison. According to a 2002 study by the Department of Justice, approximately 68 percent of criminals released from federal prison are rearrested for a felony or serious misdemeanor within three years of their release. Almost 47 percent were convicted of a new crime. Over half of those released found themselves right back in prison—either for committing a new crime or violating a condition of their release.[6]

There are examples of this in every day's newspaper. Consider, for one, convicted murderer David Maust. He has been charged with killing three teenagers after being released from prison in 1999. He got out at that time after serving just half of a thirty-five-year prison sentence for killing a fifteen-year-old boy. When he was convicted in 1981, he was already serving a five-year sentence in a Texas jail for stabbing a child.

LIBERAL LUNACY:
"Conservative anti-crime measures are too expensive."

Sure, fighting and punishing crime is expensive. But allowing criminals to run rampant is far more expensive. A crime imposes extraordinary costs on the victim, his family, his neighborhood, and society. Not only do crime victims suffer direct losses of property and income, as well as incurring medical costs, they also suffer mental anguish. For the victims of murder or rape, their lives are taken or destroyed. According to a National Institute for Justice research report, the cost of crime to victims is estimated at $450 billion annually; $426 billion of that comes from violent crimes.[7] The annual cost of rape alone to the U.S. is approximately $127 billion.[8] These costs of crime include lost earnings, public program costs, medical costs, lost quality of life, and pain and suffering. Society incurs wasted resources and citizens pay a fortune on alarm systems, guns, locks, and bars.

Crime also hurts communities. Businesses lose customers when people are scared to venture out into the neighborhood. Others are forced to charge higher prices or simply move. This translates into lost jobs and tax revenues. Crime destroys neighborhoods and real estate values—as we see from America's inner cities, where real estate values are abysmal because the neighborhoods are too dangerous to live in.

VRWC TALKING POINTS

Violent and serial criminals should be imprisoned for long periods of time to keep them from terrorizing society. When criminals are behind bars, they are not stealing your car, killing your friend, or raping your daughter.

★ Crime rates fall when society is tough on crime—long, harsh prison sentences thwart crimes by both the imprisoned criminal and the would-be criminal deterred by the real threat of a long stint in the slammer.

★ Sixty-eight percent of criminals released from federal prison are rearrested for a felony or serious misdemeanor within three years of their release.

★ A 1990 study by the National Institute of Justice finds that "the average inmate costs society between $172,000 and $2,364,000 per year while *outside* prison."[9]

★ Steven Levitt of the Harvard Society of Fellows studied the effect of prison population on crime rates and found that for every one prisoner reduction, the total number of crimes committed increases by about fifteen per year.

FORGET THE ELECTRIC CHAIR, BRING ON THE ELECTRIC BLEACHERS: THE CASE FOR THE DEATH PENALTY

Liberals say the death penalty is cruel and unusual punishment—inhumane and should never be done. So ask a liberal: Did Adolf Hitler deserve the death penalty or counseling?

★ ★ ★ ★ ★

Here's what the liberals say. . .

LIBERAL LUNACY:
"The death penalty is inhumane and 'cruel and unusual.'"

The death penalty is neither inhumane nor "cruel and unusual." The U.S. Constitution specifically refers to the death penalty in the Fifth Amendment, which mentions a "capital crime" and the deprivation of "life." And except for about four years in the mid–1970s (when the Supreme Court was caught in a stranglehold of liberalism), the Court has repeatedly upheld the authority of the government to execute murderers. What's inhumane and "cruel and unusual" is the suggestion that the murderer's life is more valuable than the victim's. After all, death by lethal injection looks pretty good next to some of the ways in which murderers kill their victims—such as the eleven-year-old girl raped by four men and then killed when they stuffed her panties down her throat.[1]

The death penalty for murder isn't "cruel and unusual;" it's a punishment that fits the crime. If a person intentionally takes the life of another, he should die. "Executing a murderer," says ever-insightful pundit Don Feder, "is the only way to adequately express our horror at the taking of an innocent life. Nothing else suffices...A murderer sentenced to life in prison without the possibility of parole can still laugh, learn, and love, listen to music and read, form friendships, and do the thousand and one things (mundane and sublime) forever foreclosed to his victims."[2]

LIBERAL LUNACY:
"The death penalty doesn't deter crime."

Who cares if the death penalty deters crime? A murderer deserves to die because he himself decided to surrender his own life when he took someone else's life. He did not respect another's life, so we should not respect his. Executions permanently remove from society extremely dangerous criminals. We want these evildoers removed from our world and we want to eliminate any risk of them communicating with or having any influence on society. Political scientist John McAdams eloquently explained that "[i]f we execute murderers and there is in fact no deterrent effect, we have killed a bunch of murderers. If we fail to execute murderers, and doing so would in fact have deterred other murders, we have allowed the killing of a bunch of innocent victims. I would much rather risk the former. This, to me, is not a

Murder by the numbers

- 15,000 people are murdered every year in America. Liberals should worry more about these people, and the loved ones they leave behind, than about the murderers.

- In a 2003 Gallup poll, 74 percent of Americans supported the death penalty. In that same poll, it was shown "that most people accept the idea that an innocent person might be executed — many believe it has happened at some point in the last five years — but still support capital punishment."

- A recent ABCNews.com poll found that 65 percent of Americans support the death penalty.

- 75 percent of Americans favored executing Oklahoma City bomber Timothy McVeigh.

tough call."[3] In fact, deterrence isn't the main justification for the death penalty. But it's clear that the death penalty really does deter crime. The recidivism rate among executed murderers is a perfect zero percent.

Not convinced yet? Consider the infamous serial rapist and murderer John Wayne Gacy. Gacy was executed in 1994 for murdering thirty-three people, mostly teenage boys. Before he committed any of those murders, he had been convicted of violently raping and sodomizing a teenage boy. He was sentenced to ten years in prison, but served only eighteen months—it was 1970, the high point of liberal lunacy running amok in the justice system. Obviously, if Gacy had been put out of commission after the first crime, thirty-three men would be alive today. Often, murderers who are imprisoned and released kill again. If society had executed these criminals the first time they went to jail, the later murders would never have happened.

LIBERAL LUNACY:
"We should follow Europe's example in abolishing the death penalty."

Should we really worry about what Europeans think, let alone model our behavior after them? Many Europeans allied themselves with Hitler. Many opposed the overthrow of Saddam Hussein. Europeans sat idly by while neighboring Slobodan Milosevic's Serbian armies slaughtered and raped Croats and Bosnians. They also eat snails and frogs.

Americans place a greater value on life, liberty, and the pursuit of happiness than do most other folks around the world. Americans recognize that a murderer has sadistically taken from his victim life, liberty, and opportunity to pursue happiness. Recognizing the pain and loss

> ### CONSERVATIVES SAY IT BEST...
>
> Conservative columnist Don Feder writes:
>
> "Executing a murderer is the only way to adequately express our horror at the taking of an innocent life. Nothing else suffices...A murderer sentenced to life in prison without the possibility of parole can still laugh, learn, and love, listen to music and read, form friendships, and do the thousand and one things (mundane and sublime) forever foreclosed to his victims. "

imposed by the murderer upon the victim and the victim's survivors, Americans rightly agree that the murderer has by his own actions surrendered his own right to life. If someone shows no respect for the lives of others, why should we respect his? That other countries are more sympathetic to murderers should not influence us: if other countries choose to devalue the lives of their crime victims, that doesn't mean that we should too.

LIBERAL LUNACY:
"The application of the death penalty results in a disproportionate number of minorities being executed as compared to whites."

To conclude that something is applied "disproportionately," you must first know what would be "proportional." Liberals, please tell us exactly how many (pardon me while I slip into liberal-speak) Hispanic-Americans, Asian-Americans, Martian-Americans, Red Sox Fan-Americans, and Fatso-Americans should be sentenced to death to ensure that only a "proportionate" number of each group are being executed.

The numbers of executions are disproportionate because the numbers of crimes are too. The unpleasant fact is that more blacks and Hispanics commit crimes than do whites. Between 1976 and 1999, blacks committed 51.5 percent of the murders in the U.S.; whites committed 46.5 percent. Yet the Bureau of Justice Statistics states: "Since the death penalty was reinstated by the Supreme Court in 1976, white inmates have made up more than half of the number under sentence of death."[4] In 2002, of those persons executed, fifty-three were white and eighteen black. In 2000, forty-nine of the eighty-five people executed were white.[5] Thus, despite committing over half the murders in the U.S., black murderers are still less likely than white murders to be sentenced to death.

LIBERAL LUNACY:
"Every execution risks
killing an innocent person."

Yes, and every time you cross a street, you may get killed by a person driving somewhere to buy a loaf of bread. Just because an action risks an innocent life doesn't automatically justify eliminating that activity. Should we ban cars because of the risk of accidental deaths?

Liberals can't name a single innocent person executed in the U.S. If such a person ever existed, there is no doubt that the name would be as famous in the U.S. today as Jesus, Elvis, or J. Lo. The media would never shut up about the fact that an innocent person was executed and that "by the way, Republicans are responsible because they support the death penalty."

Liberals breathlessly point to cases in which appellate courts reversed a trial court's decision to sentence a person to death. However, most of these "reversals" resulted from technical legal errors; they didn't constitute a declaration that the convicted murderer was innocent. The best evidence the liberals can muster for this argument is that the use of DNA testing has resulted in the release of some convicts from death row. But these releases actually support keeping the death penalty. The advent of DNA testing now gives us an even greater guarantee that in the future a person convicted of murder is in fact a murderer.

LIBERAL LUNACY:
"Life imprisonment is just as bad a punishment as death."

Obviously, this is not true. If life behind bars is equivalent to death, why do so many criminals agree to plead guilty in exchange for the prosecution agreeing not to seek the death penalty? Even if someone is behind bars, he can pray, read, write, play sports, fall in love, get married, go on the Internet, and even make money. In December 1993, with only a few months to live, John Wayne Gacy taped a message for his own lucrative 900 number and continued to sell his own paintings.

VRWC TALKING POINTS

A murderer deserves to die because he himself decided to surrender his own life when he took someone else's life. He did not respect another's life, so we should not respect his.

★ The Fifth Amendment to the U.S. Constitution expressly contemplates the death penalty in America.

★ Executions permanently remove from society extremely dangerous criminals. We want these evildoers removed from our world and we want to eliminate any risk of them communicating with or having any influence on society.

★ Ample legal safeguards exist to protect the innocent from execution. Before a murderer can be executed, he must be indicted by a grand jury, and then tried, convicted, and sentenced to death by a jury overseen by a judge. Then, several years of appeals follow, allowing lawyers to investigate and reinvestigate every fact of the case.

★ Fact: 15,000 people are murdered every year in the U.S. and they each deserve to have their killer brought to justice.

★ The death penalty is not "cruel or unusual;" it's a punishment that fits the crime.

★ Who cares if the death penalty deters future crimes? If it deters future crimes, that's great; if it does not, then all we have done is killed a "bunch of murderers."[6]

OH, AND AL?
BUSH WON

Liberals just won't let the 2000 election go. The votes have been counted and recounted and the result is always the same: Bush won.

★ ★ ★ ★ ★

Here's what the liberals say. . .

LIBERAL LUNACY:
"The Republicans stole the 2000 presidential election."

No matter how many times Democrats close their eyes, click their heels, and repeat this, it will never become true. Unlike Democrats, who will do anything to win, Republicans have a long history of not challenging questionable elections. Richard Nixon lost in 1960 but didn't challenge the result—despite serious and credible allegations that Democratic operatives had engaged in fraud to fix the tallies in Texas and Illinois, giving Kennedy enough electoral votes to win.

In 2000, then–Missouri senator John Ashcroft lost an election to Mel Carnahan, who had been killed in an airplane crash a few weeks before the election. Because the death occurred so close to the election, Carnahan's name couldn't be removed from the ballot. However, Missouri's Democratic governor promised to appoint Carnahan's wife, Jean, to fill the seat if the deceased Carnahan should win. In an obvious outpouring of sympathy, the deceased Mel Carnahan won—even though he didn't quite meet the Constitutional requirements for a candidate for Senate: candidates must be at least thirty years old, U.S. citizens for at least nine years, and residents of the state when elected. I doubt that even a liberal court would find that a dead man could be considered to be either a "person" or a "citizen." But instead of challenging the election, Ashcroft conceded.

What about Bush and Gore? Did you know that in 2000, Gore "won" New Mexico by 366 votes, but Bush didn't challenge the result? Nor did Bush say anything about close Gore victories in Wisconsin and Oregon. But when Bush beat Gore in Florida by a few hundred votes—as confirmed by several recounts—all hell broke loose. But despite a herculean effort by the liberal media and a liberal activist Florida Supreme Court to give Al Gore Florida's electoral votes and the 2000 presidential election, George Bush gained more votes than Gore on election night after the original count, the automatic recount, and after the absentee ballots were counted. Bush was never behind; how exactly did he steal an election in which he won the original count and all the recounts?

Also, the media's decision to call Florida for Gore before that state's polls closed cost Bush thousands of votes. With over one hour remaining before the polls closed in the ten heavily Republican Florida counties, ABC, CNN, FOX News, CBS, MSNBC, and NBC all incorrectly declared that Gore had won Florida's twenty-five electoral votes. This cost Bush thousands of votes. Why go out to vote if the election is already decided?

American Enterprise Institute scholar John R. Lott, Jr. explains, "Polling conducted after the election indicates that the media had an impact on voter behavior, and that the perception of Democratic wins discouraged Republican voters."

Three different studies reached this same conclusion. A survey of western panhandle Florida voters conducted by the Republican polling company John McLaughlin & Associates estimated that the media's early call for Gore cost Bush about 10,000 votes. Similarly, Lott concluded that, "By prematurely declaring Gore the winner shortly before polls had closed in Florida's conservative western panhandle, the media ended up suppressing the Republican vote." Using voting data for presidential elections from 1976 to 2000, Lott controlled for a variety of factors affecting turnout and found that Bush received "as many as 7,500 to 10,000 fewer votes than he would normally have expected."[1] Even Democratic strategist Bob Beckel determined that Bush lost up to 8,000 votes in the Florida panhandle after Florida was called for Gore.

It's also interesting to note that on October 30, 2000, a then–unknown woman, Katherine Harris, Florida's secretary of state, sent a letter to the news networks imploring them not to call a winner in Florida until after the polls— including the polls in Florida's western panhandle—had closed. Harris wrote, "The last thing we need is to have our citizens in the Central Time Zone think their vote doesn't count—because it certainly does!"[2]

LIBERAL LUNACY:
"Al Gore just wanted every vote counted."

Well, Al Gore got his wish—twice! Every voter in Florida had his or her vote counted—twice! In reality, it was Al

Gore who tried to steal the election. Al Gore became the first presidential candidate in history to concede an election, only to then call back and say "just kidding." He pleaded to have "every vote count," while seeking to prevent just that. Let-Every-Vote-Count Gore tried to disenfranchise American servicemen serving overseas by going to court to disallow military absentee ballots. Democratic operatives even issued a five-page memo describing exactly how to disqualify military ballots. Gore said he wanted "every vote counted," but immediately after the election he didn't ask for a statewide recount. He only wanted the votes in three heavily Democratic counties to be recounted. Why didn't Gore ask for a recount in all sixty-seven Florida counties?

Six million Floridians voted in the 2000 presidential election. Contrary to what liberals want you to believe, all of them had their votes counted more than once: when they were first run through the voting machines, then again when each vote was reread as required by Florida's automatic recount statute (which kicked in due to the closeness of the election).

LIBERAL LUNACY:
"The U.S. Supreme Court gave the election to Bush."

Wrong again. Liberals often conveniently downplay the fact that seven of the nine Supreme Court justices ruled that the state-wide manual recount violated Floridians' constitutional rights by not defining what would constitute a valid "vote" during the recount. Liberal justices David Souter and Stephen Breyer, as well as maddeningly moderate justices Sandra Day O'Connor and Anthony Kennedy, all found that Florida's proposed manual recount violated the U.S. Constitution. Also, the U.S.

Supreme Court absolutely had the legal authority to intervene into the Florida debacle. The election of the president and vice president of the United States is a federal issue. Indeed, the only elected positions in our democratic republic for which the entire citizenry may cast a vote are the president and vice president. The U.S. Constitution specifically sets forth the method by which the president and vice president are to be elected. The Constitution provides that the state legislature—not the state supreme court—is responsible for creating the process whereby the state's electors are to be selected.

> ### CONVERSATION STOPPER
>
> How exactly did Bush steal an election when he won all the recounts?
>
> George Bush gained more votes than Al Gore on election night after the automatic recount and after the absentee ballots were counted.

The Florida Supreme Court had overstepped its bounds in violation of the Constitution, and the U.S. Supreme Court intervened to save the day.

LIBERAL LUNACY:
"Americans are enraged at Republican chicanery, and will make them pay at the ballot box."

Oh yeah? If the Republican "theft" of the 2000 election is such a hot campaign issue, why did the Republicans buck history in the 2002 midterms, picking up seats in the House and the Senate? How did George's brother Jeb Bush—despite campaigning by Al Gore, Bill Clinton, and Jesse Jackson—manage to eke out a nineteen-point reelection win as Florida's governor? Why did presidential election lightning rod Katherine Harris get elected to

Congress? Sure looks as if the country is with the Republicans on this one.

Obviously, to the extent Americans were "split" about who should be president in 2000, by 2002 they had made up their minds.

VRWC TALKING POINTS

Every Florida voter had his or her vote counted—at least twice. Consider:

* Despite pretending to "want every vote counted," Al Gore tried to disqualify votes by American servicemen serving overseas. Gore also sought recounts in three heavily Democratic counties instead of a state-wide recount.

* ABC, CNN, FOX News, CBS, MSNBC, and NBC all incorrectly declared a Gore victory in Florida—with over an hour still left before the polls closed in ten heavily Republican counties. Democratic strategist Bob Beckel estimates that this may have cost Bush up to 8,000 votes.

* Seven of the nine U.S. Supreme Court justices, in addition to the chief judge of the Florida Supreme Court, found that the Florida Supreme Court's ordered state-wide recount violated the Constitution. Two of the U.S. Supreme Court justices finding the constitutional violations were Bill Clinton appointees.

* If the public believed that George Bush and the Republicans stole the 2000 presidential election, then how come the Republicans bucked history in the 2002 midterm elections by gaining control of the U.S. Senate, adding to their control of the U.S. House of Representatives, reelecting Florida governor Jeb Bush

by a nineteen-point margin, and electing Katherine Harris to the U.S. House?

VRWC ACTION KIT

Economist John Maynard Keynes once said, "The ideas of economists and political philosophers, both when they are right and when they are wrong, are more powerful than is commonly understood. Indeed, the world is ruled by little else. Practical men, who believe themselves to be quite exempt from any intellectual influences, are usually the slaves of some defunct economist. Madmen in authority, who hear voices in the air, are distilling their frenzy from some academic scribbler of a few years back."

Who are the economists, political philosophers, and academic scribblers of the modern conservative movement? There are many, and the list is growing.

This book is the product of reading conservative authors, attending lectures and debates, watching political shows on television or listening to them on the radio, and my own personal experiences debating liberals in New York City and on television. Because the *Handbook* is not intended to be a definitive work on any of the issues addressed, here is a list of resources and information that I have found helpful in staying abreast of Conspiracy developments.

INSPIRATIONAL INDIVIDUALS

In addition to conservative politicians and their advisors, there are hundreds of intelligent and articulate conservative commentators. Here is a list of those individuals whom I have found particularly interesting and persuasive. I pay attention when I see articles by these folks and when they appear on my television. On particular points, these commentators may disagree with me and I with them. That's okay. Often, you can learn much from listening to and communicating with those with whom you disagree.

Bill Bennett, former U.S. Secretary of Education, bestselling author, and head of the public policy group Empower America. Bennett always offers an intelligent view, though he is particularly good on education and foreign policy issues.

Judge Robert Bork, former federal judge, professor of law, bestselling author, and scholar at the American Enterprise Institute. Bork's views on the state of American law are particularly insightful.

Brent Bozell, president of the Media Research Center and one of the nation's foremost experts on liberal bias in the media.

Patrick Buchanan, longtime columnist, former presidential candidate, telegenic talk-show host, and articulate defender of the America First movement.

William F. Buckley, Jr., raconteur, founder of the influential *National Review* magazine, bestselling author, and one of the earliest conservatives on television with PBS's *Firing Line.*

Kellyanne Conway, founder, president, and CEO of the Washington, D.C.–based "The Polling Company," conservative commentator, and one of the "Fifty Most Powerful Women in Politics," according to *Ladies' Home Journal.*

Ann Coulter, perhaps the second most famous woman (after Hillary) in American politics today. Coulter is an attorney, bestselling author, and conservative diva who sets the standard against which all other conservative commentators should be compared.

Monica Crowley, FOX News Channel political analyst, successful author, Richard Nixon scholar, and radio show host.

Matt Drudge, founder and operator of the Drudge Report (*www.drudgereport.com*), the nation's best website for the most up-to-date news and political gossip.

Dinesh D'Souza, research fellow at the Hoover Institution, bestselling author, true American success story, and definitely a person with whom you would want to serve on a college Republican newspaper.

Larry Elder, Los Angeles–based radio talk-show host known as the "Sage from South Central" who debunks popular liberal myths every day, as well as in his excellent book, *The Ten Things You Can't Say in America.*

Richard Epstein, law professor, author, and clearly one of the smartest people in the world, with the ability to explain theoretically yet clearly the most complicated legal and political issues.

Don Feder, columnist, author, radio talk-show host and all-around talented conservative pundit.

Steve Forbes, editor and president of the free market–oriented *Forbes* magazine and former presidential candidate, who brought the idea of a "flat rate income tax" into the mainstream.

Milton Friedman, a true intellectual giant whose résumé includes a Nobel Prize in economics. Friedman is second to none in his ability to defend the benefits of the free market and is the intellectual father of the school choice movement.

John Fund, intelligent conservative pundit who writes editorials for the *Wall Street Journal* and collaborated with Rush Limbaugh on the bestseller *The Way Things Ought to Be.*

Frank Gaffney, founder of the Center for Security Policy and an insightful commentator on American foreign policy and defense issues.

Robert George, standup comedian and editorial writer for the *New York Post*.

Jonah Goldberg, Lucianne's son and a darn funny writer for *National Review Online*.

Lucianne Goldberg, founder of the popular website *www.lucianne.com*, former New York literary agent, mom of Jonah, and hated by liberals (but loved by conservatives) for her role in helping prove Bill Clinton's felonious perjury in the Paula Jones/Monica Lewinsky affairs.

Mark Helprin, author and excellent writer for the Claremont Institute and the *Wall Street Journal*.

Sean Hannity, media superstar, radio talk-show host, bestselling author, and co-host of FOX News Channel's hit television show "Hannity & Colmes."

David Horowitz, successful author, intellectual bomb-thrower, brilliant political strategist, and a man who understands the application of the "art of war" to politics and how Republicans should use it.

Laura Ingraham, attorney, bestselling author, and media star, with her own nationally syndicated radio show.

William Kristol, author and editor of the *Weekly Standard* magazine. Kristol is an influential conservative in print, in the lecture hall, and on the airwaves.

David Kopel, author and research director at the Independence Institute, and author of numerous outstanding pieces explaining why guns are good.

Michael Ledeen, author and scholar at the American Enterprise Institute. Ledeen understands what it will take to destroy international terrorism and its supporters.

David Limbaugh, attorney, bestselling author, and nationally syndicated columnist whose recent book,

Persecution: How Liberals are Waging War against Christianity, is an eye-opener—even for Ayn Rand libertarians.

Rush Limbaugh, mega media superstar, bestselling author, and radio host who has single-handedly given more liberals heart attacks than tobacco, fatty foods, and alcohol combined.

John R. Lott, Jr., statistician, former professor of law, and now resident scholar at the American Enterprise Institute. Lott is the author of *More Guns, Less Crime: Understanding Crime and Gun Control Laws*, the definitive book of how guns in America save far more lives than criminals using guns take.

Rich Lowry, editor of *National Review* and author of the now-definitive history book of the Clinton era, *Legacy: Paying the Price for the Clinton Years.*

Joel Mowbray, syndicated columnist and author of *Dangerous Diplomacy: How the State Department Threatens America's Security.* Mowbray shocked the nation with his discovery that of the fifteen visas available for the 9/11 hijackers, all should have been rejected.

Stephen Moore, economist and president of the Club for Growth. Moore is an articulate, passionate spokesperson and political activist for less government, free markets, and tax cuts.

Dick Morris, yes, Morris worked for Bill Clinton, but his political analysis on the FOX News Channel is second to none. Morris has been a strong critic of Hillary Rodham Clinton, thus earning him at least an honorable mention from the VRWC.

Deroy Murdock, influential New York–based nationally syndicated columnist and columnist for *National Review Online.*

Charles Murray, author of several influential books, including the groundbreaking *Losing Ground*, which showed how government welfare programs actually hurt America's poor.

Benjamin Netanyahu, the most eloquent and intelligent defender of Israel and the defense strategy of destroying terrorists instead of pandering to them.

Grover Norquist, Republican activist extraordinaire, whose work as president for Americans for Tax Reform is just part of his overall plan to make the Republican Party into the majority party for decades to come.

Oliver North, war hero, bestselling author, columnist, television and radio star, and almost-U.S. senator. Simply put, North is a great American hero.

Walter Olson, author, Manhattan Institute scholar, and founder of the influential website *www.overlawyered.com*, a fantastic resource for research, facts, and anecdotes about how the law and lawyers are dragging down America.

Bill O'Reilly, bestselling author and straight-talking, common sense–advocating host of top-ranked television show *The O'Reilly Factor.*

Richard Poe, bestselling author of *Seven Myths of Gun Control* and founder of the blogsite *www.richardpoe.com.*

Mark Skousen, unique and entertaining free market economist who writes the financial newsletter *Mark Skousen's Forecasts and Strategies.*

Thomas Sowell, author, columnist, and fellow at the Hoover Institution. Sowell's columns and books are absolutely always must-reads.

John Stossel, a free market libertarian and gadfly to the liberal media who anchors *The John Stossel Specials* for ABC News and frequently appears on ABC's *20/20.* Stossel's produced programs are must-sees and are always worth watching—even taping.

Phylis Schlafly, one of the most extraordinary women of the twentieth century, who single-handedly led the movement to stop the liberal's Holy Grail, the Equal Rights Amendment.

R. Emmett "Bob" Tyrrell, Jr., founder and editor-in-chief of *The American Spectator* magazine and author of *Madame Hillary: The Dark Road to the White House.*

Eugene Volokh, young and energetic legal intellectual, prolific writer, and professor of law at UCLA Law School.

Walter Williams, professor, economist, author, columnist, and occasional host of Rush Limbaugh's radio show. Williams's writings are always must-reads.

George Will, author, columnist, and longtime conservative pundit on Sunday morning talk shows.

MAGAZINES AND NEWSPAPERS

American Enterprise	*National Review*
American Spectator	*New York Post*
America's First Freedom	*New York Sun*
City Journal	*Reason Magazine*
Claremont Review of Books	*Wall Street Journal*
Conservative Chronicle	*Washington Times*
Human Events	*Weekly Standard*
Freeman: Life and Liberty?	

CONSERVATIVE THINK TANKS, ORGANIZATIONS, AND WEBSITES

Conservatives have experienced so much political success over the last decade in part because of their ability to circumvent the information flow gushing from the liberal-controlled media, public schools, and universities. And how have conservatives been able to circumvent these liberal monoliths? Two major reasons are the rise of the Internet and the ever-growing import of outstanding conservative think tanks. The combination of research and analysis from conservative think tanks, with their ability to use the Internet and cable news to communicate their opinions to the public, provides critical information to conservative politicians, conservative media folks, and even conservative college students under siege at liberal universities. No more are Americans forced to choose between the "moderate" liberals at NBC News and the "socialists" of National Public Radio.

Over the years, I have found the following conservative and libertarian organizations and think tanks to offer many intelligent arguments, facts, and opinions against liberalism. For anyone interested in learning more about how to defeat liberals, familiarity with the following groups and their websites is invaluable.

American Conservative Union, *www.conservative.org.* Longtime grassroots conservative political organization that sponsors the annual CPAC convention and supports capitalism, a strong national defense, traditional moral values, and interpreting the Constitution according to the original intent of the Framers.

American Enterprise Institute, *www.aei.org.* Think tank devoted to free markets, limited government, and strong national defense.

American Life League, *www.all.org.* Outstanding and influential pro-life organization.

Americans for Tax Reform, *www.atr.org.* Influential antitax organization run by grassroots organizer extraordinaire Grover Norquist.

Atlantic Legal Foundation, *www.atlanticlegal.org.* New York–based public interest law firm advancing cause of limited government, free enterprise, and sound (i.e., not junk) science.

CATO Institute, *www.cato.org.* Leading libertarian think tank advocating less government, free markets, and the protection of property rights.

Center for Individual Rights, *www.cir-usa.org.* Leading conservative public interest law firm.

Center for the Study of Popular Culture, *www.cspc.org.* Scholar David Horowitz's organization dedicated to advancing the cause of America and conservatism; publishes the influential *FrontPage Magazine* at *www.frontpagemag.com.*

Club for Growth, *www.clubforgrowth.org.* Political organization devoted to helping elect antitax, limited government, and pro-economic growth politicians adhering to the economic views espoused by President Ronald Reagan.

Competitive Enterprise Institute, *www.cei.org.* Think tank devoted to free enterprise and limited government.

Defenders of Property Rights, *www.yourpropertyrights.org.* Public interest law firm dedicated to preserving individual property rights and restoring the Fifth Amendment's Takings Clause in America.

Empower America, *www.empoweramerica.org.* Bill Bennett's organization dedicated to educational reform, a strong national defense, free markets, and Social Security reform.

Federalist Society for Law and Public Policy Studies, *www.fed-soc.org.* The premier organization in the nation for conservative attorneys who believe that judges should interpret, but not make, laws.

Foundation for Economics Education (FEE), *www.fee.org.* The nation's oldest organization dedicated to advancing free markets, limited government, and free trade.

Foundation for Individual Rights in Education (FIRE), *www.thefire.org.* Dedicated to ridding America's universities of the censorship arising from political correctness and radical liberalism.

Free Congress Foundation, *www.freecongress.org.* A politically and culturally conservative influential organization

Gun Owners of America, *www.gunowners.org.* Aggressive pro–gun rights organization.

Heartland Institute, *www.heartland.org.* Chicago-based organization advocating school choice, free market solutions to environmental issues, privatization, and deregulation; publisher of the outstanding publication *Environment and Climate News,* which advocates common-sense environmentalism.

Heritage Foundation, *www.heritage.org.* Powerful and influential conservative think tank.

Hoover Institution, *www-hoover.stanford.edu.* One of the most influential intellectual institutions in the world, with preeminent scholars such as economists Milton Friedman and Thomas Sowell.

Independent Women's Forum, *www.iwf.org.* A conservative antidote to liberal feminists, the IWF proves that truly strong, smart, and independent woman need not toe America's radical liberal agenda.

Institute for Humane Studies, *www.theihs.org.* Located at George Mason University in Virginia, the IHS helps college and graduate students learn about free markets and individual liberty.

Institute for Justice, *www.ij.org.* Free market–oriented public interest law firm well known for successfully litigating for school choice programs and against silly government regulations.

Intercollegiate Studies Institute (ISI), *www.isi.org.* Works to educate students about the classical foundations of individual liberty.

Landmark Legal Foundation, *www.landmarklegal.org.* Well-known free market conservative-oriented public interest law firm.

Leadership Institute, *www.leadershipinstitute.org.* Premier organization dedicated to training young conservatives to be future leaders of the conservative movement.

Manhattan Institute for Policy Research, *www.manhattan-institute.org.* Longtime influential conservative think tank based in New York City. The Manhattan Institute offers an impressive array of scholars articulating conservative and free market solutions to urban problems.

Media Research Center, *www.mediaresearch.org.* "America's media watchdog" devoted to documenting the liberal bias in the mainstream media.

National Federation of Independent Business, *www.nfib.com.* The political lobbying organization on behalf of America's small businesses, for free enterprise and free markets, and against intrusive government interference in the economy.

National Legal Center for Public Interest, *www.nlcpi.org.* A law foundation dedicated to fostering knowledge about the law and justice in a society committed to free enterprise, property rights, and individual rights.

National Rifle Association, *www.nra.org.* One of the most influential and powerful organizations (at least I hope so) in the nation, with three million members dedicated to preserving the Second Amendment and the individual right to own guns.

National Taxpayers Union, *www.ntu.org.* Influential anti-tax organization.

Pacific Legal Foundation, *www.pacificlegal.org.* West Coast–based public interest law firm advancing causes of free enterprise and individual property rights while fighting intrusive government regulations and policies based upon "junk" environmental science.

Southeastern Legal Foundation, *www.southeasternlegal.org.* Atlanta-based public interest law firm advancing the causes of limited government, individual economic freedom, and the free enterprise system.

Washington Legal Foundation, *www.wlf.org.* A public-interest legal center that uses lawsuits and publications to advance the causes of free enterprise, property rights, a strong national defense, and a fair civil and criminal justice system.

IMPORTANT BOOKS

Anderson, James H., *The Citizen's Guide to Missile Defense* (Washington, D.C.: The Heritage Foundation, 1999). Short yet outstanding primer on America's need for missile defense.

Antonelli, Angela, "The Environment: Promoting Community-Based Stewardship," *Issues 2000: The Candidate's Briefing Book* (Washington, D.C.: The Heritage Foundation, 2000).

Bailey, Ronald (editor), *Global Warming and Other Eco-Myths: How the Environmental Movement Uses False Science to Scare Us to Death* (New York: Prima Publishing, 2002). An excellent book written by many experts who debunk numerous myths about the purportedly "dangerous state of the environment."

Bastiat, Frederic, *The Law: The Classic Blueprint for a Just Society* (Irvington, NY: Foundation for Economic Education, 1998). First published in 1850 by the author, who explains in this long essay how to think about individual liberty and government in a free society.

Bennett, William J., *Why We Fight—Moral Clarity and the War on Terrorism* (Washington, D.C.: Regnery, 2003). Justifies both the war on terror and the war in Iraq.

Biswnanger, Harry, (editor) *The Ayn Rand Lexicon: Objectivism from A to Z* (New York: Penguin, 1986.)

Bolick, Clint, *Voucher Wars: Waging the Legal Battle over School Choice* (Washington, D.C.: Cato Institute, 2003). The case for school choice discussed in the context of Bolick's litigation on behalf of the cause.

Bork, Robert H., *Coercing Virtue: The Worldwide Rule of Judges* (Washington, D.C.: AEI, 2003). How judges in the United States and abroad seek to take decision-making from the democratic and political processes.

Bork, Robert H, *Slouching Towards Gomorrah—Modern Liberalism and American Decline* (New York: ReganBooks/ HarperCollins, 1996). Chronicles the debasement of American culture.

Bork, Robert H., *The Tempting of America—The Political Seduction of the Law* (New York: Simon & Schuster, 1990). Explains the dangers of judges making law and usurping the democratic political process.

Coulter, Ann, *High Crimes and Misdeameanors: The Case Against Bill Clinton* (Washington, D.C.: Regnery, 1999). Why Bill Clinton deserved to be impeached.

Coulter, Ann, *Slander: Liberal Lies about the American Right* (New York: Crown, 2002). How liberals control the mass media and advance liberalism by lying about conservatives.

Coulter, Ann, *Treason: Liberal Treachery from the Cold War to the War on Terrorism* (New York: Crown Forum, 2003). How liberals keep siding against the United States.

Courtois, Stephane, et al., *The Black Book of Communism: Crimes, Terror, Repression* (Cambridge, MA: Harvard University Press, 1997). A tome analyzing the archives of the former Soviet bloc and showing how Soviet communism led to terror, murder, and repression; in short, a vindication of Reagan's belief that the Soviet Union was an "evil empire."

Crier, Catherine, *The Case against Lawyers* (New York: Broadway Books, 2002). An eloquent indictment of the current criminal and civil justice systems.

D'Souza, Dinesh, *Letters to a Young Conservative* (New York: Basic Books, 2002). An excellent primer on conservative thought, written in the thoroughly enjoyable style of C. S. Lewis's *The Screwtape Letters*.

D'Souza, Dinesh, *Ronald Reagan: How an Ordinary Man Became an Extraordinary Leader* (New York: Simon & Schuster, 1997). A fun and informative discussion of the man who won the Cold War and revived America's greatness.

D'Souza, Dinesh, *What's So Great About America* (Washington, D.C.: Regnery, 2002). Defends the U.S. against liberal attacks by multiculturalists and anti-American liberals.

Dershowitz, Alan *The Case for Israel* (New York: John Wiley & Sons, 2003). Dershowitz puts his lawyerly skills to good use in making the case for Israel and battling back the typical anti-Israel arguments.

Elder, Larry, *Showdown: Confronting Bias, Lies, and Special Interests that Divide America* (Irvine, CA: Griffin, 2003). A continued attack on liberal myths.

Elder, Larry, *The Ten Things You Can't Say In America* (New York: St. Martin's Press, 2000). A fun attack on popular liberal myths.

Friedman, Milton, *Capitalism and Freedom* (Chicago: University of Chicago Press, 1962). An eloquent defense of free markets and individual economic freedom, written in a more scholarly style than *Free to Choose*.

Friedman, Milton and Rose Friedman, *Free to Choose: A Personal Statement* (New York: Harcourt, 1980). An eloquent defense of free markets and individual economic freedom.

Furchtgott-Roth, Diana and Christine Stolba, *Women's Figures: An Illustrated Guide to the Economic Progress of Women in America* (Washington, D.C.: The AEI Press and Independent Women's Forum, 1999). An outstanding resource and treasure trove of key facts and statistics about the status of women in America.

Goldberg, Bernard, *Bias:A CBS Insider Exposes How the Media Distort the News* (Washington, D.C.: Regnery, 2002). An insightful and eye-opening account of the career dangers of straying from the liberal agenda as a reporter for CBS News.

Hannity, Sean, *Let Freedom Ring:Winning the War of Liberty over Liberalism* (New York: ReganBooks, 2002). A clear and concise argument against liberalism in a world at war with terrorism.

Hayek, F. A., *The Road to Serfdom* (Chicago: University of Chicago Press, 1944). The case against the rise of big-government socialism in the twentieth century.

Horowitz, David, *How to Beat the Democrats And Other Subversive Ideas* (Dallas: Spence Publishing Company, 2002). A clear vision about how conservatives can win at the ballot box by a true political genius.

Horowitz, David, *How the Left Undermined America's Security* (Washington, D.C.: Center for the Study of Popular Culture, 2002). A great, concise, and detailed case about how liberals and their policies undermined America's national security, leading to 9/11.

Howard, Philip, *The Death of Common Sense: How Law is Suffocating America* (New York: Random House, 1994). A great book about how regulations suffocate American business and American life.

Huber, Peter W., *Hard Green: Saving The Environment From the Environmentalists—A Conservative Manifesto* (New York: Basic Books, 1999). Makes the case for free market environmentalism.

Huber, Peter W., *Liability: The Legal Revolution and its Consequences* (New York: Basic Books, 1988). Explains how tort law is changing America.

Ingraham, Laura, *The Hillary Trap: Looking For Power In All The Wrong Places* (New York: Hyperion, 2000). The case against Hillary Rodham Clinton and her vision of women in America.

Ingraham, Laura, *Shut Up & Sing: How Elites from Hollywood, Politics, and the UN Are Subverting America* (Washington, D.C.: Regnery, 2003). A fun and irreverent look at liberal elites in all their forms.

Kent, Phil, *The Dark Side of Liberalism: Unchaining the Truth* (Augusta, GA: Harbor House, 2003) A clear and concise attack on liberalism.

LaPierre, Wayne and James Jay Baker, *Shooting Straight: Telling The Truth About Guns In America* (Washington, D.C.: Regnery, 2002). Defends the Second Amendment and gun ownership in America against liberals seeking to use the 9/11 attacks to confiscate guns.

Lomborg, Bjørn, *The Skeptical Environmentalist: Measuring the Real State of the World.* (Cambridge: Cambridge University Press, 2001). If you read only one book about liberal environmentalist myths and the falsity of their prognostications about the state of the world, this is the book; no book better debunks the flawed science and flawed record of liberal doomsday predictions than this one, written by a Danish statistics professor.

Kaplan, Lawrence and William Kristol, *The War Over Iraq: Saddam's Tyranny and America's Mission* (San Francisco: Encounter Books, 2003. A scholarly yet accessible case for invading Iraq.

Ledeen, Michael, *The War Against the Terror Masters: Why it Happened. Where We Are Now. How We'll Win* (New York: St. Martin's Press, 2002). A detailed account of how Middle

Eastern nations provide terrorist organizations with the infra-structure needed to carry out terrorist attacks on civilization.

Lewis, Bernard, *The Crisis of Islam: Holy War and Unholy Terror* (New York: Random House, 2003). A great, clear explanation of the Islamic world and its views of the Western world.

Lieberman, Myron, *The Teacher Unions: How they Sabotage Educational Reform and Why* (San Francisco: Encounter Books, 2000). Describes the growth of teacher unions and how they work to thwart educational reform.

Limbaugh, David, *Persecution: How Liberals Are Waging War Against Christianity* (Washington, D.C.: Regnery, 2003). The bestselling book detailing how liberals attack Christianity.

Limbaugh, Rush, *The Way Things Ought To Be* (New York: Pocket Books, 1992). An irreverent, persuasive, and fact-filled case against liberalism.

Lott, John R., Jr., *The Bias Against Guns: Why Almost Everything You've Heard About Gun Control Is Wrong* (Washington, D.C.: Regnery, 2003). How guns save lives and how the media refuses to report this fact.

Lott, John R., Jr., *More Guns, Less Crime: Understanding Crime and Gun Control Laws* (Chicago: University of Chicago Press, 1998). The famous statistical case for encouraging widespread gun ownership in America.

MacDonald, Heather, *Are Cops Racist?* (Chicago: Ivan R. Dee, 2003) Debunks the myth of "racial profiling" in America.

Moe, Terry M., *Schools, Vouchers, and the American Public* (Washington, D.C.: Brookings Institution Press, 2001). Explains how the American public views school voucher proposals.

Moore, Stephen and Julian L. Simon, *It's Getting Better All the Time: The Greatest Trends of the Last 100 Years* (Washington, D.C.: Cato Institute, 2000). An outstanding resource full of invaluable statistics and data showing the amazing contributions to humankind the U.S.'s devotion to free markets and individual liberty has endowed upon this society.

Murray, Charles, *Losing Ground: American Social Policy 1950–1980* (New York: HarperCollins, 1984). The famous case against government welfare.

Read, Leonard, *Anything That's Peaceful* (Irvington, NY: Foundation for Economic Education, 1998). Originally published in 1964, Read explains in easy-to-understand language the libertarian, free market view of the economic world.

Sammon, Bill, *At Any Cost: How Al Gore Tried to Steal the Election,* (Washington, D.C.: Regnery, 2001). A straightforward account of how the liberal media and Al Gore tried to steal Florida from George Bush.

Sanera, Michael and Jane S. Shaw, *Facts, Not Fear: Teaching Children about the Environment* (Washington, D.C.: Regnery, 1999). A valuable primer on environmental issues from a non-hysterical, non-sky is falling view.

Schlafly, Phyllis, *Feminist Fantasies* (Dallas: Spence Publishing Company, 2003). Essays articulating the case against radical feminism, with an outstanding foreword by Ann Coulter describing the amazing life of Phyllis Schlafly.

Sowell, Thomas, *Controversial Essays* (Stanford, CA: Hoover Institution Press, 2002). If Sowell writes it, it's a must-read, and this book of essays is no exception.

Stroup, Richard L., *Eco-nomics: What Everyone Should Know About Economics and the Environment* (Washington, D.C.: Cato Institute, 2003). Discusses free market environmentalism.

Tanner, Michael D., *The Poverty of Welfare: Helping Others in the Civil Society* (Washington, D.C.: Cato Institute, 2003). Criticizes government welfare and while discussing the role of private philanthropy and charity in combating poverty.

Weaver, Henry Grady, *The Mainspring of Human Progress* (Irvington, NY: The Foundation for Economic Education, 1997). Originally published in 1947, this easy-to-read, common-sense book discusses the role of business and technology in advancing human societies.

Will, George F., *Suddenly* (New York: Macmillan, 1990). A compilation of Will's essays, including fascinating ones concerning Robert Bork's nomination to the U.S. Supreme Court.

Williams, Walter E., *More Liberty Means Less Government: Our Founders Knew This Well* (Stanford, CA: Hoover Institution Press, 1999). A compilation of must-read essays defending human liberty and criticizing government by one of America's most intelligent and lucid writers.

Williams, Walter E., *Do the Right Thing* (Stanford, CA: Hoover Institution Press, 1995). Another must-read compilation.

ACKNOWLEDGMENTS

I would like to acknowledge Ann Coulter, Leonard Leo, Gene Meyer, Robert Hornak, Rick Rubinstein, Emily Barsh, Rhoda Dunn, Dee Fonseca, Sammi Gavich, Jay Shellhorn, David Shapiro, Dr. David Berube, Tim Valliere, and Dan Goldman—all of whom assisted with this project or in my professional life in critical ways at critical times over the years. Noelle Kowalczyk deserves a special place of honor for being such an outstanding editor of the manuscript.

A special thanks is also owed to the Honorable Kenneth W. Starr for inspiring me as my law professor and role model. I must also thank my literary agent Gene Brissie (and Lucianne Goldberg for putting me in touch with Gene), as well as Joe Giganti and Stella Harrison. Extra kudos go to Joe and the American Life League for educating me on the abortion issue. I must also thank my lawyers, who are also my friends, Frank Martinez and Sal Calabrese.

Finally, I would like to thank my many, many friends and colleagues (both liberal and conservative) who have worked and played with me for the last decade here in New York City. Without their patience in hearing me out about why they should own guns and vote against tax-hiking, big-government liberals like Hillary Rodham Clinton, this book could not have been written.

NOTES

Chapter 2: No Liberal Media Bias? Let's Get Real

1   Ann Coulter, *Slander: Liberal Lies and the American Right* (New York: Three Rivers Press, 2002), 71.

2   John Heilemann, "The Truth, the Whole Truth, and Nothing But the Truth," *Wired*, November 2000, 264.

3   Coulter, 144.

4   Ibid., 71.

5   Bill Sammon, *At Any Cost* (Washington, D.C.: Regnery, 2001), 41.

6   Coulter, 109.

7   Wayne LaPierre and James Jay Baker, *Shooting Straight: Telling the Truth about Guns in America* (Washington: Regnery, 2002), 22.

8   John R. Lott, Jr., "Why People Fear Guns," January 3, 2004, FOX News Channel, http://www.foxmarketwire.com/story/0,2933,107274,00.html

Chapter 4: The War in Iraq: Saddam Had It Coming

1   The White House, "A Decade of Deception and Defiance." http://www.whitehouse.gov/infocus/iraq/decade/book.html

2   Ibid.

3   Ibid.

4   Contents based on the October 9, 2003, press conference of Paul Bremer, Coalition Provisional Authority Administrator.

5   President William J. Clinton, Address to the Nation on the Bombing of Iraq, December 16, 1998.

6   The White House, "A Decade of Deception and Defraud."

Chapter 5: The Best Way to Give Peace a Chance in Iraq: Keep the U.S. Military Kicking Butt

1 http://www.whitehouse.gov/omb/budget/fy2005/overview.html

2 Ibid.

3 http://www.gpoaccess.gov/usbudget/fy00/pdf/budget.pdf

Chapter 6: Who Would Osama Vote For?

1 President George W. Bush, The White House, The National Security of the United States of America, September 17, 2002.

2 Benjamin Netanyahu, "The Case for Toppling Saddam," Wall Street Journal, September 20, 2002.

3 Democrats for National Security, www.demsfornatsec.org, Ronald D. Asmus and Jeremy D. Rosner, "It's National Security, Stupid," DLC, Blueprint Magazine, April 15, 2003.

Chapter 7: Want Sanity and Civilization in the Middle East? Support Israel

1 David Horowitz, The War Room, Vol. 3, #3, "Axis of Evil," April 2, 2002.

2 World-Reuters, "Poll: majority of Palestinians Back Suicide Bombing," October 19, 2003, http://news.yahoo.com/news?tmpl=story2tv=/nm/20031019/w/_nm/mideast_palestinian.

3 from What Islam Is About by Yahiya Emerick. Cited in Robert Spencer, Onward Muslim Soldiers (Washington, D.C.: Regnery, 2003), 17.

4 Ibid.

5 From the book Deen al-Haqq, financed by Saudi royalty, cited in Spencer, 17.

6 Ibid.

Chapter 8: Helplessness Is Not a Virtue: Why We Need Missile Defense

1 Brian T. Kennedy, "Defending the West: Current Debate over Ballistic Missile Defense," On Principle, vol. 9 no. 3 June 2001, Claremont Institute.

2 300,000 people were killed at Hiroshima and Nagasaki.

3 Jim Wolf, "U.S. Hits Target in Sea-based Missile Test," Reuters, December 12, 2003.

4 James H. Anderson, The Citizen's Guide to Missile Defense (Washington, D.C.: The Heritage Foundation, 1999).

5 The White House, National Security Presidential Directive/NSPD-23, December 16, 2002.

6 Testimony of David B. Rivkin, Jr. and Lee A. Casey before U.S. Senate Foreign Relations Committee, May 25, 1999. "[T]he ABM Treaty no longer binds the United States as a matter of international or domestic law. This is because the Soviet Union disappeared in 1991, rendering performance of the ABM Treaty as originally agreed impossible."

7 Jack Spencer, "Lifting the Limits on Missile Defense," March 30, 2000. The Heritage Foundation. http://www.heritage.org/Press/Commentary/ED033000a.cfm

Chapter 11: Get Your Laws Off my Pocketbook: Why Lower Taxes Benefit Everyone

1 Henry Hazlitt, *Economics in One Lesson* (New York: Three Rivers Press, 1988), 26.

2 Leonard E. Read, *Anything That's Peaceful* (Irvington, NY: Foundation for Economic Education, 1998), 10–11.

3 All information courtesy of Americans for Tax Reform Foundation.

4 Rush Limbaugh, *The Way Things Ought To Be* (New York: Pocket Star, 1992), 78

5 Read, *Anything That's Peaceful,* 44.

Chapter 12: Reagan vs. Clinton: Guess Who *Really* Saved the Economy?

1 Though I have heard this argument in the past, I was reminded of many of these points during a speech given by Grover Norquist of the Americans for Tax Reform Foundation, during a lecture in New York in October 2003. I have done my best to paraphrase his excellent presentation.

2 For good defenses of the Reagan economy, see also Dinesh D'Souza, *Ronald Reagan: How an Ordinary Man Became an Extraordinary Leader,* and Peter B. Sperry, Ph.D., *The Real Reagan Economic Record: Responsible and Successful Fiscal Policy.*

3 Bob Dole and Jack Kemp, *Trusting the People* (New York: HarperCollins, 1996).

4 Dinesh D'Souza, "How Reagan Reelected Clinton," *Forbes Magazine,* November 3, 1997.

Chapter 13: The Runaway Judiciary: Rule of Law, Not Rule by Judges

1 "Survey Says Personal Liability Limits Fail to Keep Pace with Growth in Household Assets," May 25, 2001, Jury Verdict Research data, http://www.insurancejournal.com/news/newswire/national/2001/05/25/14011.htm

2 Shirleen Holt, "Go Ahead, Splurge on the Bulge, but any Resulting Fat is On You," *Seattle Times*, September 8, 2003.

3 Council of Economic Advisors, "Who Pays for Tort Liability Claims? An Economic Analysis of the U.S. Tort Liability System." April 2002.

4 Senator Mark Hillman, "Outrageous Lawsuits Carry Hefty Price Tag," Colorado Senate, www.coloradosenate.com, July 28, 2003.

5 Andres Grossman, "An Expensive Growth Industry," October 9, 2003, www.townhall.com/columnists/guestcolumns/printgrossman200310096shtml.

6 Hillman, "Outrageous Lawsuits."

7 "Survey Says."

8 Hillman, "Outrageous Lawsuits Carry Hefty Price Tag."

9 Bill Winter, "Warning! Do Not Read This While Driving a Car," http://216.239. 41.104/search?q=cache:M_406q4ncmkJ:www.lp.org/lpnews/0204.

10 Council of Economic Advisors, "Who Pays for Tort Liability Claims? An Economic Analysis of the U.S. Tort Liability System," April 2002.

11 Richard A. Oppel, Jr., "Bush Enters Fray Over Malpractice," The *New York Times*, January 17, 2003.

Chapter 14: Big Government: Thanks, Hillary, but No Thanks

1 Economist Joseph Schumpeter is often credited with coining the idea of "creative destruction" in the 1940s.

2 Dinesh D'Souza, *Letters to a Young Conservative* (New York, Basic Books, 2002), 89–90.

3 Robert E. Rector, Kirk A. Johnson, and Sarah E. Youssef, "The Extent of Material Hardship and Poverty in the United States," Heritage Foundation Web memo, http://www.heritage.org/Research/welfare/wm187.cfm.

4 Robert Rector, "Welfare: Broadening the Reform," Heritage Foundation's *Issues 2000*, 293.

5 Friedrich August von Hayek.

6   Committee of Government Affairs, United States Senate, "Government at the Brink: Vol. I, Urgent Federal Government Management Problems Facing the Bush Administration" (June 2001), 1.

7   *Meyer v. Nebraska*, 262 U.S. 390 (U.S. Supreme Court 1923).

Chapter 15: Death by a Thousand Paper Cuts: How Government Regulations Are Killing You

1   Philip Howard, *Death of Common Sense: How Law Is Suffocating America* (New York: Warner Books, 1996), 14.

2   Jonathan Klick and Thomas Stratman, "First, Do No Harm," *Regulation*, Spring 2003, 9; Jonathan Klick and Thomas Stratman, "Offsetting Behavior in the Workplace," April 14, 2003.

3   Ibid.

4   Tammy O. Tengs, "Optimizing Societal Investments in the Prevention of Premature Death," doctoral dissertation, School of Public Health, Harvard University, June 1994.

5   Erin M. Hymel and Lawrence W. Whitman, "Regulation: Reining in the Federal Bureaucracy," www.heritage.org/issues/rgulation (citing Kenneth Cole, "Federal Rules Fuel the Size Gap between Trucks and Cars," *Detroit News*, March 29, 1998) see also Julie Defalco, "The Deadly Effects of Fuel Economy Standards: CAFE's Lethal Impact on Auto Safety," June 1999, http://www.cei.org/pdf/1631.pdf

6   Erin M. Hymel and Lawrence W. Whitman, "Regulation: Reining in the Federal Bureaucracy," www.heritage.org/issues/regulation

7   Ibid.

8   Angela Antonelli, Heritage Foundation, *Regulation*, 1998 Candidate's Book, Chapter 3. See Christopher Douglass, Michael Orlando, and Melinda Warren, "Regulatory Changes and Trends: An Analysis of the 1998 Budget of the United States Government," *Policy Brief* No. 182, Center for the Study of American Business, August 1997.

9   Randall Fitzgerald, *Mugged by the State: Outrageous Government Assaults on Ordinary People and their Property* (Washington, DC: Regnery, 2003). $3,017.55 per person assumes 285 million Americans.

10 The Congressional Review Act (CRA), Subtitle E of Title II (Small Business Regulatory Enforcement Fairness Act) of the Contract With America Advancement Act of 1996, established an expedited process by which Congress reviews and may disapprove any final federal agency regulation.

Data on the number of final rules are from U.S. General Accounting Office at http://www.gao.gov/decisions/majrule/majrule.htm and www.gao.gov/fedrule/fedrule2.htm. Thomas Hopkins, "Regulatory Costs in Profile," *Policy Study* No. 132, Center for the Study of American Business, August 1996.

11 Statement of Scott Moody, Senior Economist, Tax Foundation, "The Cost of Tax Compliance," before the Subcommittee on Oversight Of the Ways and Means Committee of the U.S. House of Representatives, July 17, 2001.

Chapter 16: An "Exit Strategy" for the War on Poverty: End Welfare in America

1 Centers for Disease Control, National Health Statistics, Division of Vital Statistics, Out of Wedlock Births as Percentage of All Births, 1940–1998; See Centers for Disease Control, National Health Statistics, Division of Vital Statistics, Out of Wedlock Births (http://www.cdc.gov/nchs/fastats/unmarry.htm).

2 Stephen Moore and Julian Simon, *It's Getting Better All the Time* (Washington, DC: Cato Institute, 2000), 6.

3 Robert Rector and Sarah Youssef, "How Poor Are America's Poor?" in *Intellectual Ammunition*, November 1, 1998.

4 Centers for Disease Control, National Health Statistics, Division of Vital Statistics, Out of Wedlock Births as Percentage of All Births, 1940–1998; See Centers for Disease Control, National Health Statistics, Division of Vital Statistics, Out of Wedlock Births (http://www.cdc.gov/nchs/fastats/unmarry.htm).

5 Robert E. Rector, *Means-Tested Welfare Spending: Past and Future Growth*, The Heritage Foundation, March 7, 2001.

Chapter 17: Round Up the Usual Suspects: Why Terrorist Profiling Makes Sense

1 A similar article to this chapter appeared in Mark W. Smith, "In Defense of Common Sense: The Case for Terrorist (Not Racial) Profiling," *Engage: The Journal of the Federalist Society's Practice Groups* (October 2003), Vol. 4, Issue 2.

2 Athan G. Theobarris, "Political Counterintelligence," in *Spying On Americans: Political Surveillance From Hoover To The Huston Plan I* (Philadelphis: Temple University Press, 1978). In response to the spread of the Ku Klux Klan, Attorney General Robert Kenney sent a team to Mississippi to help identify individuals involved in terrorism.

3   Max Boot, "The End of Appeasement: Bush's Opportunity to Redeem America's Past Failures in the Middle East," *The Weekly Standard*, February 10, 2003. On April 18, 1983, a Shiite suicide bomber killed sixty-three people, including seventeen Americans, and on October 23, 1983, another Shiite suicide bomber attacked the U.S. Marine barracks in Beirut, killing 241 soldiers. Also "Hezbollah Summit Presence Sends Signal?," United Press International, October 19, 2002; Walter Williams, *We Need To Profile*, at www.townhall.com/columnists/walterwilliams/ww20020612.html

4   See "*Achille Lauro* Hijacking, October 7, 1985," at www.terrorismvictims.org/terrorists/achille-lauro.html

5   Radical Muslim terrorist groups blew up Pan Am Flight 103 over Lockerbie, Scotland. Ron Wheeler Albany, "Why No Protests When Americans are Killed?," *Times Union*, March 31, 2003. "One Muslim terrorist was sentenced to life in a Scottish jail" and the "other was acquitted and returned to a hero's welcome in Tripoli." See also Williams, "We Need to Profile," note 21.

6   *Timeline: Al Qaeda's Global Context* (Public Broadcasting System), available at www.pbs.org/wgbh/pages/ frontline/shows/krew/etc/cron.html. See also Wlliams, "We Need to Profile," note 21.

7   Hezbollah attacked a Saudi National Guard facility in Riyadh in 1995, killing five Americans. Boot, *supra* note 21.

8   Radical Islamic terrorist groups bombed the U.S. embassies in Africa in 1998. See Krepinevich, note 3; Boot, note 21 ("Islamist operatives bombed . . . two U.S. embassies in Africa in 1998.").

9   "Islamist operatives bombed . . . the USS *Cole* in 2000." Boot, note 21.

10   James Traub, "The Things They Carry," *New York Times Magazine*, January 4, 2004.

11   *60 Minutes: That Dirty Little Word "Profiling"* (CBS television broadcast, December 2, 2001). Steve Kroft stated, "[U]sing race as a factor in criminal investigations is both commonplace and supported by the highest courts in the land."

12   See John Stossel, *Rethinking Racial Profiling*, ABCNews.com, October 4, 2001.

13   See *Herbert v. City of Saint Clair Shores*, 2003 U.S. App. LEXIS 4450 (6th Cir. March 11, 2003) (Krupansky, J., dissenting) stating "The targeting of a criminal suspect solely by reference to the subject's race violates the constitution." (cites omitted); *60 Minutes: That Dirty Little Word "Profiling"* (CBS television broadcast, Dec. 2, 2001) quoting Randy Means, attorney, who explained that singling out people for investigation solely on race is illegal, but noting that using race or ethnicity as one aspect of a criminal profile is legal and a valuable tool.

Chapter 18: I Have a Dream: Let's End Racial Preferences Once and For All

1   See "What the Black Man Wants: An Address Delivered in Boston, Massachusetts, on January 26, 1865, reprinted in *The Frederick Douglass Papers* 59, 68 (J. Blassingame & J. McKivigan eds. 1991). As quoted in *Grutter v. Bollinger*, U.S. Supreme Court 2003 (Thomas, J., concurring and dissenting in part.)

2   *Adarand Constructors, Inc. v. Pena*, 515 U.S. 200, U.S. Supreme Court 1995 (Thomas, J., concurring.)

Chapter 19: Melting Pot *Sí*, Multiculturalism No: Bringing Sanity to the Immigration Issue

1   Dean E. Murphy, "Imagining Life Without Illegal Immigrants," *New York Times*, January 11, 2004.

2   Stephan Dinan, "Americans Oppose Increase in Immigration," *Washington Times*, January 8, 2004.

3   Michael E. Fix and Karen Timlin, "Welfare Reform and the Devolution of Immigrant Policy," The Urban Institute, *New Federalism Issues and Options for States*, October 1997.

4   Joel Mowbray, "Visas Should Have Been Denied," *National Review*, October 9, 2002.

5   Jerry Seper, Tens of Thousands of Illegal Aliens in U.S. Are Criminals," *Washington Times*, National Weekly edition, February 2–8, 2004.

Chapter 20: Former Fetuses, Unite: Why Being Pro-Life is the Right Choice

1   See William F. Buckley, Jr., "The Eternal Problem in Abortion Debate," *National Review*, June 16, 1997.

2   Robert E. Moffit, et al., "Crime: Turning the Tide in America," *Issues '98: The Candidate's Briefing Book* (Washington, D.C.: Heritage Foundation, 1998), 234.

3   The Heritage Foundation.

4   American Life League, www.all.org.

5   Moffit, et al., "Crime: Turning the Tide in America," 234.

6   In *Slouching Toward Gomorrah*, Robert Bork discusses how his wife posed a similar question.

Chapter 21: You've Gone a Long Way Off the Deep End, Baby: Why Every Woman Should Reject Radical Feminism

1. Ben J. Wattenberg, *The Good News is the Bad News is Wrong* (Lanham, MD: Rowman & Littlefield, 1984), 182.

2. Phyllis Schlafly, Feminist Fantasies (Dallas, TX: Spence Publishing, 2003), 4.

3. Robert H. Bork, *Slouching Towards Gomorrah* (New York: Regan Books, 2003), 224.

4. Dinesh D'Souza, *Letters to a Young Conservative* (New York, Basic Books, 2002), 105.

Chapter 22: Plucking Chicken Little: A Common-Sense Approach to the Environment

1. Dinesh D'Sousa, *Letters to a Young Conservative* (New York: Basic Books, 2002).

2. Lyn Scarlet, "Make the Environment Dirtier — Recycle," *Wall Street Journal,* January 14, 1991, in *Facts, Not Fear* (Washington, D.C.: Regnery, 1999), 28.

3. Michael Sanera and Jane S. Shaw, *Facts, Not Fear: Teaching Children about the Environment* (Washington, D.C.: Regnery, 1999), 126.

4. Ibid.

5. Ibid.

6. Ibid, 128–29.

7. Thomas Gale Moore, "Warmer Earth Might be Welcome Trend," April 28, 1998, http://www.cato.org/cgi-bin/scripts/printtech.cgi/dailys/4-28-98.html.

8. Norman E. Borlaug and Michael Senera, "Feeding a World of 10 Billion People: The Miracle Ahead," in *Global Warming and Other Eco-Myths: How the Environmental Movement Uses False Science to Scare Us to Death* (Ronald Bailey, ed., Prima Publishing 2002), 30.

9. Bjørn Lomborg, *The Skeptical Environmentalist* (Oxford: Cambridge University Press, 2001), 4.

10. Ibid, 5.

11. Ibid, 6.

Chapter 23: Don't Let Hillary Choose Your Ob/Gyn: The Case Against Government-Controlled Health Care

1 Elena Cherney, "Universal Care: Has a Big Price: Patients Wait," *Wall Street Journal*, November 12, 2003 (quoting Dr. Lee Errett, chief of cardiac surgery at St. Michael's Hospital).

2 See The Emergency Medical Treatment and Active Labor Act (42 U.S.C.S. 1395dd) (referred to colloquially as the "Patient Dumping" Act).

3 Cherney, "Universal Care Has a Big Price."

4 James Frogue, "A High Price for Patients: An Update on Government Health Care in Britain and Canada," The Heritage Foundation Backgrounder #1398, www.heritage.org/Research/HealtCare/BG1398.cfm

Chapter 24: Stopp Supprting Publik Skools: Defending School Choice

1 Linda Chavez, "D.C. Schools a Disgrace," February 5, 2003, www.townhall.com

2 Milton Friedman interview, CNBC, March 24, 2003, Milton and Rose D. Friedman Foundation at www.friedmanfoundation.org.

3 David W. Kirkpatrick, "Alternative Teacher Organizations: Evaluation of Professional Associations," Policy Study No. 231, September 1997. www.rppi.org/education/p5231.html.

4 Myron Lieberman, *The Teacher Unions: How They Sabotage Education Reform and Why*, (New York: Encounter Books, 2000).

5 Clint Bolick, *Voucher Wars* (Washington, D.C.: Cato Institute, 2003), 1.

6 Jennifer Garrett, "School Choice: A Lesson in Hypocrisy," The Heritage Foundation, June 26, 2002.

8 Brief Amicus Curiae of National Association of Independent Schools in Support of Petitioners in *Zelman v. Harris*, Nos. 00-1751, 00-1777, 00-1779 (U.S. Supreme Court 2000 Term), 1.

9 Libby Sternberg, "Lessons from Vermont: 132-Year-Old Voucher Program Rebuts Critics," Cato Institute Briefing Papers (September 10, 2001), 1.

11 Terry Moe, *Schools, Vouchers, and the American Public*, (Washington D.C.: Brookings Institution, 2001), 164.

12 Garrett, "School Choice."

13 See U.S. Dept. of Commerce, Bureau of Census, Statistical Abstract of the United States 140 (2001) (Table 218).

Chapter 25: Guns Don't Kill People: Liberal Gun Control Laws Kill People

1   *U.S. v. Verdugo-Urquidez*, 494 U.S. 259 (1990).

2   John R. Lott, Jr., *More Guns, Less Crime: Understanding Crime and Gun Control Laws*, 2nd Edition (Chicago and London: The University of Chicago Press, 2000), 219.

3   Findings from the Task Force on Community Preventive Services, "First Reports Evaluating the Effectiveness of Strategies for Preventing Violence: Firearms Laws," Mortality and Morbidity Weekly Report, October 3, 2003 (at http://www.cdc.gov/mmwr/preview/mmwrhtml/rr5214a2.htm).

4   John R. Lott, Jr., *The Bias Against Guns: Why Almost Everything You've Heard About Gun Control is Wrong* (Washington, DC: Regnery 2003), 83.

5   John R. Lott, Jr., *The Bias Against Guns: Why Almost Everything You've Heard About Gun Control is Wrong* (Washington, D.C., Regnery, 2003), 83–84.

6   Wayne LaPierre and James Jay Baker, Shooting Straight: Telling the Truth about Guns in America (Washington, D.C., Regnery, 2002), 41.

Chapter 26: It's Simple: Do the Crime, Serve the Time

1   U.S. Department of Justice, Bureau of Justice Statistics, Prisoners in 1990, NCJ-129198, May 1991, 7.

2   Robert E. Moffit, et al., "Crime: Turning the Tide in America," *Issues '98: The Candidate's Briefing Book* (Washington, D.C.: Heritage Foundation 1998), 231 (citing U.S. Department of Justice, Bureau of Justice Statistics, Sourcebook of Criminal Justice Statistics, 1996).

3   U.S. Department of Justice, Bureau of Justice Statistics, Prisoners in 1994, NCJ-151654, August 1995, 1.

4   Stephen Hayward, "Broken Cities: Liberalism's Urban Legacy," *Policy Review*, March/April 1998, 18.

5   Moffit, et al., "Crime: Turning the Tide in America," 234 (citing Cheryl Ringel, "Criminal Victimization 1996," Bureau of Justice Statistics. NCJ-165812. November 1997, 4–6; and National Crime and Victimization Survey (NCVS) and Uniform Crime Reports).

6   U.S. Department of Justice, "Recidivism of Prisoners Released in 1994," June 2002, NCJ 193427 (http://www.ojp.usdoj.gov/bjs/pub/pdf/rpr94.pdf).

7   Ted R. Miller, et al., National Institute of Justice Research Report, "Victim Costs and Consequences: A New Look," January 1996, 1.

8 Ibid.

9 David P. Cavanaugh and Mark A. R. Kleiman, *A Cost-Benefit Analysis of Prison Cell-Construction and Alternative Sanctions*, National Institute of Justice, May 1990.

Chapter 27: Forget the Electric Chair—Bring on the Electric Bleachers: The Case for the Death Penalty

1 See *Collins* v. *Collins*, 510 v.s. 1141 (U.S. Supreme Court, 1994) (Scalia, J. concurring).

2 Don Feder, "McVeigh Puts Capital Punishment in Focus," www.townhall.com/columnists/donfeder/printdf20010425.shtml, April 25, 2001.

3 John McAdams, Professor, Marquette University, at www.prodeathpenalty.com

4 U.S. Department of Justice, Bureau of Justice Statistics, http://www.ojp.usdoj.gov/bjs/cp.htm

5 Ibid.

6 John McAdams, Professor, Marquette University, at www.prodeathpenalty.com

Chapter 28: Oh, and Al? Bush Won

1 John R. Lott, Jr., "Let the Sunshine In," *NationalReviewOnline*, December 10, 2003 (http://www.nationalreview.com/comment/lott200312100915.asp).

2 Bill Sammon, *At Any Cost* (Washington, D.C., Regnery, 2001), 32–33.

BIG DISCOUNTS ON EXTRA COPIES
Help Keep the Conspiracy Going Strong!

Please consider ordering extra copies at bulk discounts for friends, business and social associates, local political groups, radio talk-show hosts, and newspaper editors.

To order multiple copies of *The Official Handbook of the Vast Right-Wing Conspiracy*, consult the discount schedule below and call 202-216-0601, ext. 430.

Special Bulk Copy Discount Schedule	
10–24 copies	20% OFF!
25-49 copies	35% OFF!
50-99 copies	40% OFF!
100-199 copies	45% OFF!
200 or more...	Call

Since 1947
REGNERY PUBLISHING, INC.
An Eagle Publishing Company • Washington, DC